A HISTORY
OF
BLACK BAPTISTS
IN THE
UNITED STATES

WILLIAM L. BANKS

B.A., University of Pennsylvania
B.D., Lincoln Seminary
M. Th. and D. Min.,
Eastern Baptist Theological Seminary

ISBN 978-0-7414-2738-0

Published by:

INFINITY
PUBLISHING.COM
1094 New De Haven Street, Suite 100
West Conshohocken, PA 19428-2713
Info@buybooksontheweb.com
www.buybooksontheweb.com
Toll-free (877) BUY BOOK
Local Phone (610) 941-9999
Fax (610) 941-9959

Printed in the United States of America
Published August 2013

TABLE OF CONTENTS

INTRODUCTION

Historians and history teachers must take more seriously the role played by black Americans in the religious life of America. Perhaps we should omit the word *religious*, for it remains difficult for some Christians to see any dichotomy between the sacred and the secular. To teach American history adequately, mention must be made of the profound influence of a people whose roots run deep in American soil; blacks have been in this country for more than four centuries. Myrdal (124) estimates that slightly more than 27 percent of American blacks have Native American blood (cf. Herskovits, 133f).

Slavery, of course, had a tremendous moral, economic and political impact, one that remains felt to this day. Recall that the Methodists split in 1844, the Baptists divided in 1845, and the Presbyterians separated in 1861 over the slavery issue. Think of the cost of the Civil War in terms of lives lost, property destroyed, sectionalism nurtured; how is it possible to teach the history of the United States and ignore the part played by blacks?

Racism—as it showed itself in the Reconstruction era, in the rise of the Ku Klux Klan, lynching, gerrymandering, grandfather clauses, poll taxes, Jim Crow laws—was and still is destructive, a waste of talent and money. It is a stench in the nostrils of God, for He is no respecter of faces or races; He made from *one* (man, blood, piece of dirt) all the nations of men to dwell on all the face of the earth. [1]

The Christian interested in history appreciates seeing the hand of Jesus Christ, the Lord of History, working in the lives of blacks who accepted the Gospel. White believers who genuinely desire to help saints of color achieve their goals and fulfill their dreams, must study what is called the Black Church (Brunner, 80) and "come to grips with Black history and Black emotional interpretation of it" (Parvin, 90).

Furthermore, it is not possible to understand the Southern white man's religion apart from the religion of the black man (Mathews, 185). Whites are encouraged not to let their sense of guilt, their wish that they had acted differently in our common past, blind them to the achievements of the blacks. Look past the failure of the whites, and see the accomplishments of the blacks! The neglect of white historians at this point creates a false image of blacks, and furthers the myth of black inferiority (Roberts, 18).

Another obstacle to the proper study of the history of the black church is the absurd idea, born of racism and impossible to demonstrate, that African forms of worship express Christianity *less* well or *less* faithfully than European forms. Those who hold this concept make the value judgment that the morality, spirituality, and church life of the slaves would have been or should have been the same as that of the white man. Mathews (186, 226) decries such thinking, and suggests that the black slaves actually achieved a superior religious maturity: "Enslaved, they sang of freedom, defeated, they awaited victory: powerless, they exercised the power of the righteous remnant."

Slavery is an ugly chapter in our history. Damages wrought by this heinous practice—lost gifts, broken families, economic loss, poverty, ignorance, stigma and damaged self-esteem, cruelty, immorality, poor health, illiteracy, political chicanery, the deadening effects of paternalism, misuse of the Bible to support slavery, shame brought on the Name of Christ and His Church, and race hatred—are incalculable. Sow to the wind, reap the whirlwind remains ever true.[2]

Black slaves had no legal rights. Family life was devastated. Sexual abuse of female slaves was common. One only has to see the number of light-skin black Americans to realize the degree of miscegenation perpetrated by unscrupulous, lascivious white men; less than twenty-five percent of black Americans are of pure African blood. What good could come out of such a system?

We answer, "What you meant unto us for evil, God has turned into our good."[3] Blacks have long been a despised minority, but a Sovereign God uses that which is despised for His own glory. Whites then must not think so highly of themselves as to fail to give credit to the slaves and to their

7

descendants who helped build this great nation.[4] Any attempt to teach American History and at the same time ignore the contributions made by black Americans is unwise. Their labor, loyalty and devotion in time of war; their inventions, music, athletic prowess and achievements; their patience in their struggle for civil rights, justice, full democracy and first-class citizenship; their sense of humor, and religious fervor are noteworthy. Any omission of their contributions leaves the students of history with a picture that is lopsided, inadequate, and blind to the good hand of the God of History in the life of America.

Notes

1. Deut 10:17; II Chron 19:7; Luke 20:21; Acts 10:34; Rom 2:11; Gal 2:6; Eph 6:9; Col 3:25; I Pet 1:17; Acts 17:26.

2. Hosea 8:7. Cf. William L. Banks, *Bible and Black Slavery in the U.S.* (Haverford, PA.: Infinity, 1999).

3. Gen 50:20

4. I highly recommend Ira Berlin's *Many Thousands Gone – First Two Centuries of Slavery in North America.* Cambridge, Mass.; The Belknap Press of Harvard University Press, 1998.

CHAPTER 1

EARLIEST BAPTIST BEGINNINGS

Roger Williams

A clergyman named John Smyth, a member of the Church of England, went to the Netherlands about 1607, along with other English exiles. While in Holland, a group of these exiles established a Baptist Church. When a schism took place, some of the members returned to England to set up a Baptist church there in 1611. Some years later, some of the members also came to America.

In 1631, a Puritan minister, a graduate of Cambridge, named Roger Williams arrived at Massachusetts Bay. He was not a Baptist when he landed on these shores; he had no connection with the aforementioned English Baptists. Like most of those who fled their homeland to worship as they pleased, he had no room for those who dissented from what the Puritans considered true worship. Concerned about the voluntary choice in religion, and finding believer's baptism appealing to him, Williams became a Baptist; and joined a group of English Baptists who had come to America for refuge. In March of 1639, a former member of the Salem church pastored by Williams soon after he arrived in America, named Ezekiel Holliman, baptized Williams.

Roger Williams then baptized ten other people; with this group, he organized the first Baptist church in the New World, in Providence, Rhode Island, in 1639. Some scholars contend that John Clarke in Newport, Rhode Island, founded the first Baptist church in America in 1648 and that "Roger Williams was never a Baptist" (Adlam & Graves, 36).[1] Williams soon despaired of finding the true Church of Christ on earth. Convinced that his baptism was not in the apostolic succession, he left the Baptists and became a "Seeker."

Growth of the Baptists

The Baptists increased in Puritan New England. Their rapid growth in Rhode Island soon gave birth to the denomination's first educational institution, the College of Rhode Island, in 1764. Its name was changed later to Brown University. Baptist churches appeared in Massachusetts in 1663; New York, 1669; Maine, 1682; South Carolina, 1683; Pennsylvania and New Jersey, 1684; Connecticut, 1705; New Hampshire, 1755; Virginia, 1763; Vermont, 1765, and Ohio in 1790.

A slave baptized in 1652 in a Baptist church in Newport, Rhode Island, known as "Jack, a colored man," is believed the earliest known black Baptist (Gardner, 39). In 1685, an unknown black female was immersed as a Connecticut Rogerene. Perhaps the first free black Baptist of record was Peggy Arnold. In 1719, she became a member of the Newport Seventh Day Baptist Church, there in Rhode Island. Another black man, by the name of Quassey, was in 1743 a member of record of a Baptist church in Newton, Rhode Island (Fisher, 31f). These all belonged, of course, to white-controlled churches.

The largest center of early Baptist growth was in Philadelphia, Pennsylvania. There the Philadelphia Baptist Association was established in 1707—it still exists today—and became the most influential organization in Baptist life in the country. Its Confession of 1742 became invaluable to Baptist life in America. See the pattern: Baptists had their beginnings in the New England States (Christian, 15, 24). Slowly the denomination advanced through the Middle Atlantic States. Great growth was registered in Pennsylvania because of the religious liberty of the Quaker colonies.

However, nearly one hundred years after America was settled there were only seventeen Baptist churches in the country. Baptists were not strong in the South during this period (1650-1720). In 1714, some English immigrants introduced the Baptist denomination in southeastern Virginia. Baptists in Maine came down to South Carolina in order to escape persecution. It was in Virginia that the Baptists suffered great persecution. Between 1768 and 1776, more than 40 Baptist preachers were jailed, usually charged with disturbing the peace, but the suffering served only to increase their numbers. Originally, Baptists had little to do with the Great Awakening of 1734, but they reaped great results from the revivals. Still by 1740, there were hardly 500 Baptists in the land, and these were divided.

Obstacles to the Conversion of the Slaves

Attention turns now to the black slaves. Failure to understand the background of the slaves results in failure to appreciate their survival struggles. For a minority to succeed in a society developed primarily to meet the needs of the majority is a remarkable feat. Slavery forced the blacks to turn to the church. Conversion gave them a new standing in society. What they heard and believed about Jesus Christ enabled them to adapt to adverse conditions and to survive.

The church became a training ground for different kinds of activities, not only spiritual development, but also social, political and educational. Leadership was developed in the church. To this day, many black leaders either are clergymen or closely affiliated with black churches.

Black Baptist churches came into existence under complex circumstances. Their origin was a part of the general interest in the christianization of slaves (Tyms, 107). In its beginnings, the black church was predominantly a rural institution. Slaves were concentrated on the farms in the Southland, so that the black church, like the white church, "was in its major development a rural institution" (Richardson, 4). At this point, the black church could not be labeled, "Christian." It was unorganized, mixed up with heathen practices; there was but a veneer of Christianity. Only several generations later did the black church truly become Christian (Haynes, 50f). This period, 1619-1775, begins with the year indentured black servants landed in Jamestown, Virginia; it ends with the War of Independence.

It is seen that the "history of the seventeenth century was that of religious indifference to the Negro, with isolated exceptions" (Washington, *Black Religion* 177). There are a number of reasons why comparatively few slaves were converted to Christianity during this period. (1) In general, interest in religion was at a low level in colonial times. (2) It was difficult for the few ministers to travel over sparsely settled, rough terrain in order to serve the members of their churches. (3) Not only did the Church of England have few churches, but also the ministers of those churches for the most part were not much concerned about the spiritual welfare of blacks and Indians. Indeed, extending the Gospel to Native Americans and blacks was only the secondary function of the Society for the Propagation of the Gospel in Foreign parts, organized in London in 1701.[2] They made only erratic forays against "African heathenism," and achieved little (Mathews, 188).

(4) One great obstacle to evangelism was the slave-master's lack of interest in the spiritual welfare of his slaves. If the slave master showed no concern for his *own* spiritual condition, it was unlikely that he would evince concern for the religious education of the slaves or give the preachers an open door to evangelize them. (5) There was also the fear that conversion to Christianity would interfere with slave labor. Either the slaveholder, if a Christian, would hesitate to keep in slavery his "brother," or the slaves themselves would rebel because of their "freedom" in Christ.

These were the fears held. Spiritual equality with their masters would make it harder to control the slaves. Because of such beliefs, blacks in some areas were forbidden altogether to hold any type of assembly. One example of slave control is cited in which a law was passed that a male slave who ran away for the fourth time for a period of thirty days or more was to be castrated. In 1710 a member of a Baptist church in Charleston, S. C. carried out this sentence, and the resultant controversy almost devastated the life of the congregation (Scherer, 67; W.D. Jordan, 155).

(6) Illiteracy and the lack of knowledge of the English

language also restricted evangelization. (7) The slaves' environment was not conducive to the Christian life. Indeed, plantation life was decidedly unhealthy, both physically and as concerns the development of Christian character. (8) Another matter that impeded the process of evangelism was the hostility of some whites to those whites who showed Christian sympathy to the slaves.

(9) Finally, there existed what might be broadly termed social reasons for the barriers that prevented evangelization of blacks during these colonial days. As aforementioned, the first Africans brought here were indentured servants, not slaves. However, racial prejudice soon manifested itself. Discriminatory laws were passed, and by the 1660s, slavery had gained legal status, statutory recognition in the Colonies (Shade, and Herrenkohl, 25). There were white laymen *and* preachers who saw nothing inconsistent with supporting slavery *and* Christianity. They believed that God ordained that some men should be slaves and some masters.

There were those who held that the African was not fully human. He was a savage closely related to the ape, and mentally inferior; or he had no soul and so could not be saved. In general, prior to the Revolutionary War, the policy with respect to slavery was accommodating and inconsistent. Both the French and the Spanish took time to instruct their slaves "into Popish religion to the reproach of those who profess a better" (Jones, 28). Early Baptists did not make many approaches to the slaves. Those who did, preached to them, and baptized the converts, but did not emancipate them. Haynes (46, 52) summarizes, "Before 1800 there are no historical evidences which would lead one to the position that a Negro community within American Protestantism existed."

The First Great Awakening

God granted the spiritual awakening so desperately needed. There began in the Middle Colonies in the 1720s what has been called The Great Awakening. It must not be looked at with modern eyes as if it were a well organized, superbly advertised and promoted event. It was not. There were different phases of this religious phenomenon—a separate New England phase, a Middle Colonies phase, and a Southern phase. Different denominations reached their peaks at different times. The varieties of experiences, leadership qualities, and different stages of acculturation led to uneven results across the colonies. In the New England States, the Presbyterians and Congregationalists were instrumental in the revival. Under the preaching of the Congregationalist minister, Jonathan Edwards (1703-1758), revival broke out in Northampton, Massachusetts, in 1734-1735.

Other leaders of the Great Awakening include a Dutch Reformed pastor in New Jersey, T. J. Frelinghuysen; Gilbert Tennent, a Presbyterian pastor in the same state; and George Whitefield, a traveling Methodist preacher from England, a man greatly used of God. It was not until after 1750 that the Great Awakening with its strong influence on the religious life of America contributed to the growth of the Baptists. When the revival fires had cooled in the New England States, the fire broke out anew in the South. The Baptists in North Carolina, Kentucky and Virginia were especially favored in growth.

Theologically, the Baptists were in two groups. General Baptists were Arminians, believing redemption was possible for all men. Particular Baptists were Calvinistic, believing in a limited atonement. In 1740, most of the Baptist churches in New England were Arminian in theology, and they resisted the revival because of the Calvinistic flavor. Many churches there, however, were transformed, and the Calvinist group increased. Influence of the Great Awakening was longer in the South, continuing there from the 1740s until the War of Independence (Handy, 93f).

By 1765, the main denominations were just about on the same ideological level, ready to make political progress together (McLoughlin, 60). Blacks converted to the Baptist denomination throughout the Great Awakening (Tyms, 106). In fact, the Baptists received out of the Great Awakening more members than any other denomination. Naturally, as the white Baptists grew in numbers, so the blacks grew, for they followed their owners. Sobel (98, 187) called the period just before the War of Independence one of "radical White Baptist outreach." Blacks attended and participated very early in the revivals, so that it is difficult to find a pre-black pattern of behavior. Their presence enhanced the emotional excitement of the meetings.

Presbyterians, Methodists and Baptists readily accepted the slave converts as members of their respective churches. We see the beneficial humanitarian effect of the Great Awakening in the numbers of slaves set free because of the revivals. Attempts also were made to educate the converts. Although the Baptists and Presbyterians churches did not oppose slaveholders, individual members of these denominations did come out strongly against the system. However, there were not many attempts to organize an antislavery movement (Haynes, 111). On the other hand, the Methodists officially denounced slavery and vigorously sought an end to the institution. John Wesley wrote in 1774 in his work entitled, *Thoughts upon Slavery*:

> It cannot be that either war or contract can give any man such a property in another as he has in his sheep and oxen, much less is it possible that any child of man should be born a slave. Liberty is the right of every human creature as soon as he breathes the vital air; and no human law can deprive him of that right, which he derives from the law of nature (Gewehr, 242).

Understand then that one result of the Great Awakening was a more humane attitude towards the slaves. Success at ameliorating their pitiful condition served to uplift American society as a whole. To keep a man down with one's foot on his neck necessitates staying down with him. See then in the Great Awakening many practical blessings—political, social and educational—as well as the spiritual uplift, the saving of

15

souls who responded to the Gospel preached by the evangelists. It was indeed one of the most decisive epochs in the religious life of America, leaving the soul of our country remarkably changed (Hays and Steely, 24; Noll, 35).

Notes

1. Cf. Thomas N. Bicknell, *The Story of Dr. John Clarke,* (Providence, 1915).

2. Charles C. Jones, *Religious Instruction of the Negroes in the U. S.,* 8. See C. E. Pierre, "The Work of the Society for the Propagation of the Gospel in Foreign Parts among the Negroes in the Colonies," *Journal of Negro History,* 1 (Oct 1916): 349-360. Pierre claims that the Society believed no race should be denied the Gospel because of skin color, and that the organization held the conversion of blacks as important as that of whites and Indians, 349f. See also Richardson, 2.

CHAPTER 2

AN AGE OF HELPFULNESS

Attitudes towards Slavery

Immediately after the War of Independence, 1775-1783, in which the North American colonies won their freedom from Great Britain, the spiritual condition of the nation was at low ebb. However, there was still a willingness to evangelize the slaves; and the need was great, for of the approximately half million slaves in the land in 1775, no more than 25,000 were members of the black Baptist churches.

More slave owners came to believe that religious slaves were more valuable workers than non-Christian slaves were. In the minds of the whites, "Black people were undeniably eligible for heaven but not for the full benefits of the church on earth" (Scherer, 144). Some white Baptists were slave owners before 1710; many more became owners of slaves in the years following the War for *Independence*!

While there were white Baptist voices raised against slavery, they carried no weight (Smith, 53). The very government of the Baptists meant that they had no single united voice concerning the propriety or immorality of slavery. Rapid growth of a denomination composed of autonomous assemblies precluded the possibility of developing and maintaining agreement on such an issue as slavery. Some Baptist groups passed anti-slavery resolutions and even established churches that forbade members to hold slaves.

Regional associations were effective but wielded no constitutional authority. We see the policy of the powerful Philadelphia Baptist Association (PBA) in this paragraph of its minutes for October 7, 1789:

Agreeable to a recommendation in the letter from the church at Baltimore, this Association declare their high approbation of the several societies formed in the U.S. and Europe, for the gradual abolition of slavery of Africans, and for guarding against being detained or sent off as slaves, after having obtained their liberty; and do hereby recommend to the churches we represent to form similar societies, to become members thereof, and exert themselves to obtain this important object. [1]

When the issue of slavery became more volatile, the PBA became more cautious (Shaw, 113). As early as 1789, before the polarization of attitudes across the country, the PBA gave endorsement to abolitionist groups. On October 8, 1795, the following came from the Philadelphia Baptist Association:

On application for assistance to build a meetinghouse in Savannah, Georgia, large enough to admit some hundreds of blacks in the galleries, we recommend to the churches to make subscriptions or collections for the above purpose, and to forward the amount to Mr. Ustick by the 20th of November next; which Mr. Ustick is requested to convey by the first opportunity; together with a letter of condolence to the above-mentioned blacks, and our ardent wishes that Providence may interfere in their favor, at least so far, that their masters may be moved to allow them the free enjoyment of public and private worship. [2]

Still later, the Vincent Baptist Church of Chester Springs, Pennsylvania, made known its desire that the PBA flatfootedly commit itself to freeing the slaves. However, the PBA tabled the matter. As a result, in 1832, some churches near Philadelphia withdrew and created a new and independent organization (Baxter, 104).

18

The First Black Baptist Church

Satterfield (10, 12) calls this period an "Era of Helpfulness" because the Revolutionary War brought new attitudes toward the slaves. Although no effective voices against slavery were heard, the seeds were sown for the birth of many black Baptist churches. It is at the beginning of this era that the first black Baptist church in the U. S. was born. There is some dispute about this. It is believed the Silver Bluff Church of Aiken County, South Carolina, just twelve miles from Augusta, Georgia, was the first; the date given is between 1773 and 1775.[3] George Leile (Leisle or Lisle), born a slave in Virginia in 1750 or 1751 was instrumental in the founding of this church.

"Perhaps no two men stand out more prominently in the early history of the Negro church than George [Liele] and Andrew Bryan" (Davis, 119). Leile was removed to Georgia with his master, Henry Sharpe, before the Revolutionary War. Converted to Christ in 1773 or 1774, Leile began preaching. At some point between 1773 and 1775, with the help of a white deacon by the name of Walt Palmer, he organized the Silver Bluff Baptist Church in Aiken County, S. C. The first ordained black Baptist preacher in America was thus responsible for organizing the first black Baptist church in the U.S. In part, this achievement was made possible by the autonomy of the local assembly (Brooks, "Evolution" 11).

When Leile's gifts were recognized, the whites in the church to which he belonged gave him opportunities to preach. Though set free at the death of his owner, members of the Sharpe family had Leile imprisoned in an attempt to re-enslave him (Haynes, 61). After showing his papers of manumission, he was released; he then fled to Jamaica in 1783. There he established another first, the first Baptist foreign missionary from America; he founded the first Baptist church in the city of Kingston, Jamaica—many firsts for a former slave (Torbet, 353; Woodson, *Education* 85).

19

Tense Times for Black Baptists

One of the accomplishments of the Revolutionary War was disestablishment, liberation of the churches from government control. By the end of the eighteenth century, politics became the order of the day. It was as if the war liberated the minds of the colonists. The church no longer determined what and how people should think. Political ideology displaced religion. Colonialists no longer feared the Church of England (Noll, 159f). The quest for political freedom had ended. However, as noted earlier, the *religious* scene at this time was not good at all.

> At the close of the eighteenth century the prospects of Christianity in the U.S. were most deplorably unfavorable. All parties testified to this state of affairs. The Revolutionary War had brought about a great deal of license, and all classes of witnesses testify to the low state of morals (Christian, 345).

By 1800, the Baptists were the largest Protestant denomination in the U. S., with the Methodists ranking second. The persecuted Baptists had made great strides; one could see religious progress among both the blacks and the Native Americans (Latourette, 1035). How strange that in a period following the fight for freedom, whites should turn against unsupervised black churches and consider them as places for political trouble and rebellion! Whites used every means at their disposal to dominate physically, and to control the black churches economically, legally and emotionally.

Often blacks resorted to secret meetings, something that Baptist polity—lack of a central headquarters—enabled them to do. Those who participated in such clandestine services ran the risk of physical abuse as well as excommunication from the white churches. This period following the War for Independence then was one of tension for black Baptists. Political freedom was in the air, but evidently, some whites feared blacks would breathe it and react violently (Weatherford, 119f). Fear and prejudice combined to draw the church into the controversy concerning slavery, and limiting even further the liberty of the blacks. In 1800, South Carolina forbade all black religious meetings between sunset and sunrise. Because of an appeal by the Charlestown Baptist Association in 1803, an amendment permitted holding class meetings until 9 p.m. if the majority of people present were white. In 1819, another change required that only one white man be present; he was to make sure no conspiracies were developing (Wilmore, 83f). Sweet (328f) tells of an incident in the Forks of the Elkhorn Baptist Church of Kentucky. On the second Saturday of January 1807, this church charged Sister Esther Boulwares Winney on two counts. *First:* Since her conversion, she said she had never believed any Christian kept Negroes or slaves. *Second:* She was charged with saying she believed, "thousands of white people Wallowing in Hell for their treatment to Negroes—and she did not care if there was as many more." At the next church meeting, she was excluded from the body.

Black Church Attendance and Growth

During these decades under consideration, the following held true with respect to black church attendance.[4] *First:* On many plantations the slaves could attend the same churches as did their masters. Of course, the policy in general was to have segregated seating arrangements. Usually blacks were made to sit in the galleries. C. C. Jones (273f) advised the slave States not to allow blacks to have separate church buildings. The idea is for incorporation—to have the same pastor, church building, ordinances, and services at the same time. He argued that this commingling would create "a greater bond of union between" the two races with "kinder feelings," tend to "increase subordination," and promote in a higher degree the improvement" of the blacks "in piety and morality."

Second: In time and in some areas, blacks were allowed

to have their own assemblies, but white preachers were in charge. "Much of the early autonomy of these separate black churches was short-lived. By the 1820s black churches were under the supervision of white pastors" (Raboteau, 137). *Third:* Black ministers could be the preachers for the day, but whites supervised. In the South, pioneer black Baptist preachers were more successful in those areas where the plantation system was not so strong (Frazier, 24). Keep in mind that the blacks in the afternoon services could use the same church building used by the whites in the morning; alternatively, blacks used a separate church building at the same time the whites held services.

Fourth: Black preachers were in charge of the entire congregation. These freer bodies called their own pastors, chose their own officers, and joined local Baptist associations with white churches. They sent black delegates to association meetings. The development of the black Baptist churches in the North was different from their origin in the South. Victory in the War of Independence helped increase the numbers of free blacks in the North. In turn, race relations there worsened; segregation patterns appeared, assuming a variety of forms (Reimers, 11). Dissatisfied with the prejudiced behavior Northern whites practiced in the mixed churches, blacks pulled out (Sobel, 191). According to records, this was the case of the Joy Street Baptist Church in Boston, in 1805; and in the Abyssinian Baptist Church in New York City in 1808 (Childs, 42).

As the black population in Philadelphia grew, there was an increased frequency of expressions of race prejudice. The predominantly white church to which blacks belonged employed on a number of occasions Southern white Baptist preachers who encouraged the congregation to keep the question of slavery in its "proper place." In other words, consider slavery as a political issue, one outside the domain of the church. The blacks left and in 1809 organized the First African Baptist Church in Philadelphia. Similar events occurred in other cities of the North. The case with Richard Allen in Philadelphia, and the development of the African

Methodist Episcopal Church is well known. Originally, a member of the Saint George Society, Allen and others withdrew in 1787. In 1794, Bishop Francis Asbury constituted the Bethel AME Church at Philadelphia. Despite the opposition from those whites who sought to control them, the black churches grew. Neither legal or illegal nor extra-legal restraints could stop the irrepressible desire of the blacks from forming and controlling their own churches (Berlin, 69, 286). Black Baptist churches came into existence under complex circumstances. One could talk about the origination of black churches in terms of with or without permission of the whites, and in terms of motivations, prejudices, etc.

Some scholars who take a sociological and anthropological approach, suggest that if the whites had accepted and integrated blacks from the beginning, there would have been no separate, independent black churches in America. Haynes (125) suggests the origin of the black church is not theological. He agrees with Myrdal (858) that the very existence of the black church is due to caste, without which the American church would not be divided into black and white. Mays and Nicholson (224f, 278) also propose that in part the failure of American Christianity in the realm of race relations resulted in the present status of the black church. Because whites shut out the blacks from participating in American life in other areas, the blacks were forced to make the church the hub or center of their society.

The Second Great Awakening

The first Great Awakening gave thrust to the War of Independence. "The rise of democracy was preceded and foreshadowed by the rise of religious dissent, which did much to crystallize the ideas and forces back of the American Revolution" (Gewehr, 262). Rapidly increased church membership, strengthened religious life in the colonies, the movement for popular education, the rise of political democracy, stimulation of missions, and the amelioration of the terrible plight of black slaves—those were some of the major results of the tremendous religious revival. The second period of revival began in 1800. It had its birth in the trans-Appalachian valleys of Kentucky and Tennessee. Once again, as the Baptists greatly benefited by the first Great Awakening, so the momentum of this Second Awakening carried more Baptists into the South to evangelize (McLoughlin, 106f; Lumpkin, v.).

Slow in reaching the Baptists, nonetheless it remained with them longest. Indeed, it reinforced the effects of the first Great Awakening. Of course, the protracted meetings, week after week, laid "a permanent foundation for the religious expectation of the great bulk of Negroes" (Washington, *Black Religion* 195).

When the second Great Awakening hit the North, it challenged the older way of life and caused all kinds of "endless schisms and theological debates." In the South, this second revival period served to strengthen the hold of the Baptists and Methodists, making the older sects almost an invisible minority; however, they did not deal with the slavery issue. Benevolences to the blind, helping the deaf and dumb, assisting widows—these were acceptable works. If attempts were made to tamper with the social order, or rearrange slave relationships, then the average white churchman considered such deeds were unchristian misguided efforts that belonged to the political arena, not ecclesiastical circles.[5] Despite all such efforts, women, children, blacks and Indians—those least esteemed in the society—were most benefited by the revivals. The Gospel liberates.

> Whatever inclination existed to see slavery as a church issue diminished before 1820 to the point where slaveholders rarely had occasion to feel uncomfortable within the Baptist fellowship. Displeasure was more likely to fall on the person who insisted that owning human beings was a grievous sin (Scherer, 137).

Obviously, as this period (1821-1865) closed out, the seeds sown augured for a difficult time, one of increased misery for the blacks. Keep in mind that by 1820 there were more than 100,000 black Baptist church members, including independent black church members, out of a total black population of 1,782,084. Raboteau (149) concludes, "The majority of slaves, however, remained only minimally touched by Christianity by the second decade of the nineteenth century" (Cf. Scherer, 143; Jones 62).

Notes

1. Minutes of the Philadelphia Baptist Association, 1707-1807 (Michigan: Baptist Book Trust, 1976 reprint), 247.

2. PBA Minutes, 307.

3. "By the best evidence," "so far as authentic and trustworthy writers of the eighteenth century establish," it is believed Silver Bluff was the first. George E. Simpson, *Black Religions in the New World,* 230: "Perhaps the first regular Negro church organization in the United States was a Baptist church started at Williamsburg, Virginia, in 1776." Jesse L. Boyd, *History of Baptists in America Prior to 1845:* 188. Walter H. Brooks, "Priority": "a year or two before the Revolutionary War" (172f).

Miles Mark Fisher, *Short History of the Baptist Denomination:* 35f. Edward A. Freeman, *Epoch of Negro Baptists and the Foreign Mission Board, NBCUSA, Inc.* 27. Robert T. Handy, *History of the Churches in the U.S. and Canada,* 156. Leonard L. Haynes, Jr., *Negro Community within American Protestantism,,* 60. J. H. Jackson, *Story of Christian Activism: The History of the National Baptist Convention, USA, Inc.,* 22. Owen D. Pelt and Ralph L. Smith, *Story of the National Baptists,* 37. Satterfield, 7. M. C. Sernett, *Black Religion and American Evangelicalism,* 111.

James D. Tyms, *Rise of Religious Education among Negro Baptists,* 110. Carter G. Woodson, *History* 43. Lewis G. Jordan, *Negro Baptist History, USA 1750-1930,* 21: "Appears to have dated from some years previous to 1776." Brooks ("Priority" 173) adds, "a year or two before the Revolutionary War." Lincoln and Mamiya (23, 416 note 6): "Although historical records indicate that the Silver Bluff Church was established by a slave named George Leile sometime between 1773 and 1775, the cornerstone of the present church building claims a founding date of 1750 . . . The discrepancy has not yet been cleared up".

4. For more information, W. H. Brooks, "Evolution" 13-15.

5. William H. Brackney, ed., *Baptist Life and Thought: 1600-1980,* 153: "It was computed that about ten thousand were baptized and added to the Baptist churches in the course of two or three years." Cf. McLoughlin, 137.

CHAPTER 3

WHY BLACKS BECAME BAPTISTS

Two groups that rose to power during the period beginning with the latter part of the seventeenth century, and throughout the eighteenth century, were the Baptists and the Methodists. The first distinctively black churches in the U. S. were Baptist. How did this come about? There are many reasons why blacks became Baptists predominantly.[1] The reasons hold different weights or values, depending upon two major factors. First, there is the matter of the *location* of the blacks, whether North or South, settled regions or frontier, rural or urban. The second important aspect is *time*. Different dynamics held sway before the War for Independence, during the time of increased numbers of rebellions, immediately before and during the Civil War, Reconstruction, etc.

Belief in the Gospel

First, blacks became Baptists because they believed the Gospel the Baptist preachers heralded. Those who believed were saved. Of course, not all Baptists were Christians; and not all slaves became Christians. Perhaps no more than ten percent were genuine in their faith. "At the time of Emancipation probably only a minority of the Negro slaves were nominal Christians"(Myrdal, 860). "Only a minority of slaves ever became formally Christian—many never had a chance to hear the Gospel, and others resisted what to them was a white man's religion in which words of love and justice were not reflected in deeds"(Handy, 208f),

Those slaves converted to a saving knowledge of Jesus Christ found that the God of the Bible gave them freedom although they were in bondage. He gave them hope in a world of uncertainty. He gave them rest in the midst of crisis, and peace when all around them cruel men embroiled their lives in strife. Christ gave the slaves some measure of

27

stability in a world full of contradictions. The inroads made upon the lives of the blacks by the Gospel gave them direction, helped them spiritually, and until this day the impact of the Baptists is strongly felt. Christianity satisfied the religious nature of the slave. In his miserable state there was some solace. There was an otherworldly explanation of the meaning of life, and the strong belief that "Trouble don't last always."

Evangelistic Fervor

A second important reason why many blacks chose the Baptist way is the zeal of the missionary preachers in evangelism during the Great Awakening and periods of revival (Childs, 41). The Baptists and Methodists were more active than the other denominations. They worked hard to reach the blacks (Hamilton, 70; Washington, *Black Sects* 39-42; Genovese, 234). There was a need and God used these preachers to supply that need. For the most part, the Episcopalians were ineffectual in their attempts to proselytize; and Episcopalian slaveholders were seldom able to convert their slaves. Presbyterians were more successful than the Episcopalians were, but far less successful than the Baptists or the Methodists (Stampp, 372f).

Competition between the Baptists and Methodists for converts was keen, and both groups made strong appeals. "There were many points of similarity in the evangelical spirit and teachings of Methodists and Baptists. But there was also intense competition" (McLoughlin, 133f; Handy, 168). However, certain things favored the Baptists. Unlike the Methodists, there was no outside connection for the Baptists, no national headquarters. Thus, there was no need to worry about "outside agitators," bringing in unwelcome ideas and stirring up trouble, or creating church policies that were contrary to the mores of the region in which the church was established.

Hays and Steely (29) see the Baptists as especially suited for frontier evangelism, as if to suggest the frontier and the Baptist denomination were made for each other. Individualism, free form of worship, lay leadership, autonomous policy, perhaps a Baptist "frame of mind"— these all "seemed to make the Baptist Churches at home in the primitive conditions which prevailed in new territories." In their zeal, they aimed at bringing in every lost sheep, black and white alike (W.D. Jordan, 212). These evangelists believed the black slaves could be saved the same as the white man could be saved. So vigorous were their evangelistic efforts that soon after the turn of the nineteenth century the Baptists and Methodists outstripped every other denomination in the country (Goen, 50).

Spirited Preaching

A third reason concerns the preaching of the evangelists. The Baptist and Methodist preachers who sought to win souls to Christ were a hardy lot. Regard for personal purification and piety outweighed other interests. Much credit is given to them for the part they played in winning blacks to the Baptist denomination. Their aggressive proselytizing and preaching appealed greatly to the deep emotional hunger of the slaves (Washington, *Black Religion* 194; Freeman, 18).

These white preachers went everywhere. Black slaves could not travel freely; nor could free blacks in the South go where and when they pleased. Because the black preachers were limited in their travel, this restriction gave the black Baptists an advantage over the Methodists. Only after the Emancipation were black Methodists better established and able to travel more freely.

Preaching with conviction, they brought conviction, and the Spirit of God who used these men saved souls. Their sincerity, zeal, pioneering spirit, and moral integrity gave force to their individualistic, intense concentration on inward conversion. They held the attention of their hearers, the neglected, common people. Their message was simple, "unadorned English," very personal, only slightly ritualistic. Formal ritual was unappealing to the masses (Genovese, 243;

29

Richardson, 6; Myrdal, 936). There was no involved creed, articles of faith, or catechism. "Stressing the conversion experience instead of the process of religious instruction made Christianity more accessible to illiterate slaves and slaveholders alike." Preaching from the heart, without notes, and in the vernacular, their burning message overcame the handicaps of illiteracy and the lack of education (Raboteau, 132; McLoughlin, 134). Christian (192) writes,

> The Baptist preachers were without learning, without patronage, generally very poor, very plain in their dress, unrefined in their manners, awkward in their address, all of which, by their enterprising zeal and unwearied perseverance, they either turned to advantage or prevented their ill effects.

Emotionalism

A fourth reason blacks were attracted to the Baptists is emotionalism. Mathews (196f) states it is a misconception to say that blacks became Baptists (and Methodists) because these groups were more "emotional" than others were. What is important is the way in which emotion became a part of religious exercises. There is however, an element of truth in that slaves found in the worship of the denominations something that satisfied and made sense to them in their condition. Pipes (62f, 173 fn 78) contends that "it was not until the time of the emotional preaching of George Whitefield (1714-1770) that large conversions were made among the Negroes." Without a doubt, emotionalism in preaching and in worship played a big part in drawing blacks to the Baptist faith. Those denominations that placed little emphasis on the emotions failed to attract the slaves.

Of course, not every one appreciated the holy whine, or the whoop. One man is reported to have said, he "had rather go to hell than be obliged to hear a baptist in order to go to heaven" (Gewehr, 111,114). It was not uncommon at the meetings to see large groups of people who shouted, cried, laughed, danced, barked, rolled on the ground, had visions, "spoke in tongues," swayed, gesticulated, trembled, fell prostrate, jerked, etc., all thought to be evidences of the work of the Holy Spirit; or thought to be "reflexes due largely to sympathetic like-mindedness and suggestibility ... characteristic of the primitive mind in which the power of inhibition is easily overcome by a highly developed imagination and the emotions." The blacks copied what they saw and heard; the religion of the plantation black was a "faithful copy of the white man's" religion (Park, 123). The less inhibited slaves increased the already intense fervor of an unrestrained emotionalism that differed little from that among the white farmers but lasted longer in its impact (Washington, *Religion* 194f).

Sutton (35) also argues for observing the emotionalism of the time as one of the distinguishing traits of American evangelism, especially observed in the rural sections of the country, regardless of race. Myrdal (937) believes the reports of extreme emotionalism in black churches are exaggerated. Other scholars suggest emotionalism is an escape from daily oppression, a compensation for crushed ambitions, a theme emphasized by Mays. However, whites encouraged this emotionalism and attempted to control the blacks, using the church as their whip (Berlin, 300). Suffice it to say, emotionalism was an important factor in the choice of denomination. Geographical and cultural isolation of the blacks who lived in the rural South, combined with an uneducated ministry, helped the degree of emotionalism in the black church to be more intense than that of the whites. [2]

Baptist Polity: Autonomy

A fifth reason blacks were attracted to the Baptists is that each local Baptist assembly is its own sovereign body. Each church is autonomous or self-ruling. It is easy to understand how such a church government or polity (or policy), with what Genovese (234) called "organizational flexibility," would appeal to an oppressed people. Allowing blacks some modicum of self-determination helped draw blacks to the Baptist denomination. For a people long experienced at being "second class" citizens, it was heady stuff to be able to choose their own pastor, manage their own affairs without "outside" interference (Sobel, 79; Reid, 70).

Such freedom was delicious; and the autonomy made it possible for men to be ordained and thus perpetuate the denomination. As few as four Baptists, under the leadership of a preacher could organize a church congregation (Woodson, *History* 109; Powdermaker, 230). It was not difficult for untutored blacks and whites to become instant leaders on the strength of their charisma powers alone (Washington, *Anti-Blackness* 523f).

Few obstacles prevent splits by those who seek leadership and control of their own affairs. Autonomy gave the Baptists another advantage over the Methodists: Frontiers people were not likely to accept control by someone back in the city living in comfort and ease. From the black perspective, the Methodist bishops who were in control were white (Hays and Steely, 24; Freeman, 19). Keep in mind that autonomy within a black church on a plantation prior to the Civil War was limited self-rule. Congregational church polity well suited the temper of widespread plantations, for they were little societies within themselves (Latourette, 1037). While the blacks reveled in their self-government, the whites favored such decentralization because it enabled them to maintain better control over the blacks.

Because the Baptist churches were confined to small areas on the plantations, and had their total organization right there, the whites could easily know who the members were, and their leaders and preachers. With such knowledge, the whites could better determine the policies of the church. You see that ecclesiastical independence was central to the development of the religious character of the South (Du Bois, 198).

Ease of Ordination

A sixth key to the success of the Baptist denomination among the black populace was the ease with which men became preachers. At first, white Baptists encouraged and gave blacks opportunities for self-expression. They were more than willing to extend the privilege of ordination and thus to accept blacks as preachers. Formal education was seldom required by Baptist churches, and besides, resources for training ministers were lacking. Thus, poverty played a very important part in developing the ethos of the churches in the South. Poverty affected the region's ability to educate its residents. Whereas the Baptist and Methodist churches did not insist upon a well-educated ministry, the Presbyterians, Episcopalians and Congregationalists did. Though the Baptist preachers were not well educated, they knew people, they knew audiences (Washington, *Black Religion* 190; Latourette, 1037).

"Many white and black Baptists preached without ordination, and even without the formal license of a local church. This lay preaching, generally called *exhorting*, became quasi-institutionalized among blacks" (Sobel, 160). The preacher ordained by the church was to carry out the ministerial duties associated with caring for a congregation, but all the exhorter was supposed to do was exhort: incite, urge, preach (Dennard, 262, fn 61).

After the Nat Turner revolt in 1831, black preachers were banned in the South. In summary: The ease with which men could be ordained was a drawing card to the Baptist denomination. "The only criterion for a Negro Baptist preacher was his feeling of an inner call and evidence of his ability to preach."[3] And we add, his master's permission.

Egalitarianism

A seventh reason why blacks flocked to the Baptist denomination is the belief that the white Baptist (and Methodist) ministers preached a Gospel during the eighteenth century that treated both blacks and whites as equals, putting both on the same level in the South. Evangelists fostered an inclusiveness, a class-cutting that helped establish an air of freedom (Meier and Rudwick, 94; Mathews, 205; Childs, 41). Their rapport with the common people, their appeal to the poor, the downtrodden, white or black, was one of the strong points of their early colonial witness for Christ. Of course, the fight for independence had an effect here also. The Great Awakening likewise strengthened the equalitarian strain—"rapport with the common people"—of Protestantism (Goen, 50; Handy, 112).

Adaptability to new conditions on the frontier was important, and we see the efficacy of their accommodation in the gains in membership by these two denominations (Hays and Steely, 24). They moved with the population to meet the needs of the people, taking with them a theology that liberated women and children, the poor, powerless whites, the Indians, and black slaves. As one writer put it, "God was democratized," and the result was what Franklin (199) called, "The nearest thing to interracial religious fellowship that the South produced."

Both Baptists and Methodists gave the laity roles to play in the life of the church. This too appealed to a relatively disinherited people who looked for a faith that would give promise of equally sharing in all of the gifts of the Creator. The Gospel of Jesus Christ held forth just such a promise, and the Baptist way was the instrument used whereby blacks might find fulfillment. As a community of believers, each member was the equal of all other members, with equal voice (Sobel, 88). Thurman put it:

> In the Baptist denomination any man is as significant as any other. Even the head man is no longer the head man when the rest of us decide that he isn't. And this would have a special appeal to people who were terribly circumscribed everywhere else in their world (Goodwin, 535).

Such egalitarianism was in open contrast to the lifestyle common to the gentry, for example, in Virginia (McLoughlin, 94). The outward status of men was not emphasized. A Gospel with universal (catholic) dimension that moved men to believe Christ died for them as individuals (Pipes, 63; Raboteau, 148), placed blacks on a plane of equality. This equalitarianism was only temporary. Indeed, true to the Adamic nature, there were blacks who discriminated against other blacks.

Some refused to associate with other slaves whom they regarded beneath them in point of "character, color, condition, or the superior importance of their respective masters" (Bayliss, 92, fn). Divisions existed between free blacks and slaves, between rich and poor, between mulattoes or light-skin blacks and those of darker hue. There were mulatto blacks who were Episcopalians, Presbyterians, and Congregationalists who looked down their noses at the darker hued Baptists and Methodists (Lomax, 45).

Some few Southern black Baptist churches would not allow slaves to join them, and even after the Civil War, ex-slaves were not allowed to join (Sobel, 134); however, the distinction was not based upon color, but the worldview. The color line was bent momentarily but not broken (Berlin, 69). Having fitted well with the idealism of the American Revolution, in time blacks discovered that church membership was no guarantee of full equality.

Notes

1. Benjamin G. Brawley, *A Short History of the American Negro*, 157-160. Joel B. Sutton, "Spirit and Polity in a Black Primitive Baptist Church," PhD dissertation, University of N. C. at Chapel Hill, 1983, 31f. Cf. Walter L. Williams, *Black Americans and the Evangelization of Africa, 1877-1900*, 64.

2. Philip A. Bruce, *The Plantation Negro as a Freeman*, 105; Gewehr, 235; Haynes, 65.

3. Washington, *Black Religion,* 198; Mary E. Goodwin, 535. Haynes, 65; Benjamin Mays and Joseph W. Nicholson, *The Negro's Church*, 11; Kenneth K. Bailey, *Southern White Protestantism*, 7; Milton C. Sernett, *Black Religion and American Evangelicalism*, 93; Dennard, 141.

Basic to the ease of ordination is the fact that Evangelical revivalists won over the blacks by preaching an immediate conversion experience; this made the converts immediate candidates for baptism. There was no long indoctrination period (or what may be called today, *Orientation Class,* or *New Members Class*) as a prerequisite of church membership. First Corinthians 12:13 does not support such a requirement.

Cf. Raboteau, "African-Americans, Exodus, and the American Israel," 1-17 in *African-American Christianity,* Paul E. Johnson, ed.

CHAPTER 4

WHY BLACKS BECAME BAPTISTS
(continued)

Adult Water Baptism

An eighth suggestion why Baptists were successful in winning the slaves has to do with a purported fascination with baptism by immersion, that water baptism by immersion had a strong appeal to the slaves' "mystic temperament," and his desire for the spectacular. Some scholars assert the distinctive symbolism of water baptism drew the slaves, for they understood well the representation of the drowning or dying of the old man, and the rising or resurrection of the new man.[1]

Others suggest the rite was coincidental with certain intact features of African origin, especially reminding the slaves of the powerful river spirits in whom West Africans believed (Childs, 41). Crossing the river of Jordan too was a symbol of what comes after death, a concept the African slave easily understood; thus, baptism by total immersion attracted the blacks to the Baptist denomination.

The most logical thing then to do was to connect oneself with that religious group which most resembled the kinds of worship one practiced in his homeland. Other denominations, with modes of baptism other than immersion, did not draw comparable numbers of adherents. When Howard Thurman was asked if he thought baptism by total immersion took the slaves back to the river cults of Africa as taught by Herskovits (232-234), and that this was the basis of the attraction of the Baptist denomination to blacks, his response was, "No, I don't " (Goodwin, 534).

Africanisms

How much weight should one attach to what are called Africanisms, after more than four centuries? Was water baptism by immersion the real reason for the success of the Baptists, or was it the genuine interest in the spiritual welfare of the slave? Was it the ministry of love and patience exhibited by the evangelists? (Satterfield, 96). Understandably, the slaves did not travel the Middle Passage devoid of any religious heritage. They did not come here "culturally naked" (Powdermaker, xi). Not all was lost, but of necessity, a large part of their aboriginal culture became extinct. Park (116) says that the Africans left behind almost everything but their dark complexions and tropical temperaments.

Frazier (4) argues that the possibility of the slaves retaining or transmitting their African culture was extremely rare. Many factors mitigated against the transmission or survival of Africanisms: (1) Intertribal wars (2) Selection for the trade market (3) Generally young males, a poor group to bear culture (4) Dehumanizing barracoons or barracks for temporary confinement of the slaves. All of the dehumanizing factors involved in slavery served to make impossible the survival of Africanisms to the degree suggested by Herskovits. (5) The Middle Passage (6) smaller plantations gave fewer opportunities to attempt to re-establish old practices.

(7) New slaves were mixed in with the old slaves (8) Use of native languages was discouraged and prohibited; slaves were forced to learn a new language (Park, 117). (9) White supervision; whites guarded against African practices because of their fear of revolt by the slaves. (10) Destruction of the family (Frazier, 5, 10f) (11) More whites than blacks lived in the U.S. (12) There were no areas where the topography would enable escaped slaves to hide and develop a stable community (Meier and Rudwick, 18).

Frazier (3, 6) concludes; "All this tended to bring about as completely as possible a loss of the Negro's African cultural heritage." Such was the slave's break with his motherland, that it "is impossible to establish any continuity between African religious practices and the Negro Church in the U.S." The controversy over Africanisms continues. Du Bois and Herskovits argue for such survivals. Frazier, Park, and Myrdal argue against them, contending for almost total deculturization. The majority of black scholars, "especially in recent years, such as Henry H. Mitchell, Gayraud S. Wilmore, and Cecil Cone," and J. D. Roberts, "side with Du Bois and Herskovits" (Hurst 14, fn 1).

More than likely, the slaves most isolated from the whites inculcated Africanisms in their religious practices. Although the early African slaves kept varying amounts of their religious beliefs and customs as were possible in slavery, one may argue that even these diminished further for those slaves who began to preach after 1770. They were too far "dispersed to retain much of their language, myths and traditions or to keep alive their African culture" (Powdermaker, 231).

Perhaps the safest answer is, yes, there are survivals of African culture. One should not deny altogether African influences: voodooism, fetishism, certain funeral rites, the holy dance, emphasis on the oral tradition, the congregational response, emotionalism, singing, and general temper.[2] Despite the terrific shock of enslavement, it appears that the Africans were not totally stripped of their cultural heritage. Some patterns evidently persisted, indeed, were helped by slavery and the failure to include the blacks in the total life of the country.

One thing that stuck with the blacks is the idea of the unity of the sacred and the secular (Washington, *Black Sects* 29). Some things then that the Africans received from white Christians were easier to accept and assimilate than others. The African's total worldview gave him insight and ability to receive new religious discernment. Matters like conversion experience, incantational preachings, baptism, and congregational singing—these similarities in worship made easier the movement of each race to the other. "Evangelicals, however, were different from other white people. Their religious exercises were similar enough to those which Blacks valued to make the transition to Christian rites much easier" (Mathews, 192). We conclude that there are Africanisms still practiced in black churches (Roberts, 18). However, we assert there are also Europeanisms! There are both, but it depends upon the specific question asked. African idioms incorporated into the European Christian worship service include ideas about the Devil, concepts of magic, and the tendency toward emotionalism. The slave took the predominant white Christian elements, mixed in his own idioms of religious expressions and produced a black church that indeed has its own form of worship. In time, things that were similar among the blacks and whites in the early American churches became more or less pronounced as racism increased and segregation became the general rule.

Sutton's point is that "it cannot therefore be said that emotionally volatile behavior and intense physical activity is characteristically black." Racism forced the blacks to make their churches the primary sources of social cohesion, to a degree not experienced even by poor rural whites. Blacks held their slave preachers in esteem that white preachers did not enjoy (Sutton, 36-38).

They blended their African heritage with their American experience (Berlin, 299; Handy, 208). Would one dare suggest had there been no surviving Africanisms the black man would not have survived! From the amalgamation was produced a unique religious style—Baptists, but black Baptists! Do not stretch the chain between West Africa and Afro-American folk religion in an attempt to account for the preference for the Baptist denomination (Genovese, 233). Yet it is wrong to attempt to trace all the religious practices of the blacks to white Christians. The influence of the minority black slave population upon the majority white free population's culture was significant. It was not a one-way street. The blacks took much from the whites; the whites took much from the blacks. Africanisms and spiritual strivings remain, but they exist in a Euro-American context (Sobel, 98; Genovese, 210; Roberts, 27).

Perhaps some black scholars, who argue for Africanisms and a stronger connection with Africa, seek to lessen any white influences in black religious life. Such is the thrust, for example, of "Black Theology."

Is too much credit given to the "creative spirituality of

the African religions?" (Wilmore, 37). Is it accurate to speak of "Blackamerican Christianity as a point on a continuum beginning in Africa?" It depends upon one's definition of religion. Mitchell's (9f) claim that the "early slave . . . was in many ways already a Christian believer and practitioner" is simply not biblical. One should not ignore or play down the tremendous transformation, the miraculous thing that took place, called regeneration. What the Africans had did not, could not, save them. Only Christ saves. As far as salvation is concerned, Africanisms mean nothing, and neither do Europeanisms. The Bible is neither Afrocentric nor Euro-centric; it is Theocentric.

At one time men knew God (Rom 1:21). Finding traces of truth in all world religions is expected; but knowledge about proverbs, creation, the fall of man, sovereignty, one God or many gods, goodness and providence, justice and righteousness, spiritual versus the material—may be what Mitchell (11) calls "highly supportive beliefs," but there is no salvation in them. Paul did not hesitate to tell the Ephesians that prior to their acceptance of Jesus Christ they had no hope and were "without God (*atheoi*) in the world" (Eph 2:12). Nor did he hesitate to tell the Corinthians that the "things which the Gentiles sacrifice, they sacrifice to demons, and not to God" (I Cor 10:20; cf. Acts 4:12).

There is merit in the contention that the slaves took what they learned from the whites and molded it into something new—that met their own social as well as spiritual needs, and resulted in a "Negro style" of devotion and orthodoxy, a bringing to American Christianity a "unique and powerful folk element" (Wilmore, 26; Sernett, *Black Religion* 18).

Time and American influences eliminated some of these "survivals" and modified others.

The harsh realities of slave life along with the slaves' encounter with Christianity and his African heritage, helped to produce a new religious manifestation. This new religion was characterized by new forms of expressions in styles of singing,

41

praying, preaching, shouting and testifying which reflected aspects of distinct African survivals in Black life and culture as well as traits of European influence (Duncan, 189).

Prior to the Great Awakening, America was at low spiritual ebb, and there was little evangelism among those early African slaves. Once the revivals came and the Gospel was preached, supernatural transformations took place. The God of the Bible—Whose Word transcends culture in order to save men of all races and nations from sin's wages—did His work in the hearts of those enslaved in the land of the free!

Slavery and Racism

The ninth and final reason offered in answer to the question, "Why did blacks become Baptists?" centers in the very practice of slavery itself. Earlier we learned that the ease with which men were licensed or ordained to preach was one of the attractions to the Baptist faith. Another step would be to suggest there were blacks who entered the ministry because it was an opportunity for them to escape some of the drudgery and emasculation of slavery. In other words, one might say that racism and slavery were indirectly responsible for blacks becoming Baptists. The idea put forth is that if the blacks had had more freedom to exercise their gifts in wider areas of the social and economic life of America, then possibly there would not have been so many blacks claiming they were "called to preach" (Mays and Nicholson, 11).

Segregation played an important part in shaping the character of the church. Some churches seated members indiscriminately. One church in Charles City County, Virginia, allowed all "free male members" to vote. It was not until some fifty years later that church suffrage was restricted to "free white male members" (Berlin, 68). Even free blacks, like the slaves, sat in special sections of their churches. Sometimes it was the gallery, or some distant corner of the building reserved for the saints of color. Blacks greatly influenced church architecture, for often galleries were built which opened on to the street or the vestibule, but not into the main auditorium.[3] One church in Virginia painted some of the pews black. There would be no confusion there as to who would sit where.

Without segregation there would have been fewer black churches, and therefore, so the thought runs, few black Baptists. Myrdal (875) believes the "call," the chief requisite for becoming a preacher in a Baptist church, was not much more than the "manifestation of temporary hysteria or opportunistic self-inspiration" rather than a "deep soul searching." These "called" ministers tended to retain the emotional characteristic of black religion.

On the other hand, this paradox existed: The Baptists' stand against slavery also contributed to that denomination's attractiveness to the blacks. At first, when Whitefield, who owned slaves, was in Georgia, he advocated the introduction of slaves and rum into the colony as a means of improving the economy (Woodson, *History* 26). There was, however, no unanimity of opinion regarding slavery. Because of their church polity, the Baptists lacked any organized effort against the practice and did not have the antislavery punch at first, as did the Methodists. Though strongly abolitionist in the late eighteenth century, the Baptists "were not as uniform or as effective in their attack on slavery as the Methodists" (Richardson, 5). Again, because of Baptist autonomy, the matter of slavery was left to individual conscience (Gewehr, 241). An example of one 1789 Baptist Convention's declaration indicates the strong stand taken:

> Slavery is a violent depredation of the rights of nature and inconsistent with a republican government, and therefore, [we] recommend it to our brethren, to make use of their local missions to extirpate this horrid evil from the land, and pray Almighty God that our honorable legislature may have it in their power to proclaim the great jubilee

consistent with the principles of good policy (Woodson, *History* 32).

Slaves who went to church at all, went in those early days with their masters who were religiously inclined. There was prestige in attending the master's church. Some blacks saw the white man's religion as a badge of superiority, sanctioned by the white man's God. Some slaveholders of course forbade their slaves to attend any church, be it white or black. This forced the slaves to attend secret church sessions, "with or without the consent of the master, the Negro took his Christianity." (Powdermaker, 224, 228).

The point is, as the white Baptists grew in number, so the black Baptists grew in number. "Whatever the religion of the masters, the slaves, when given a chance, over-whelmingly preferred the Baptists and secondarily the Methodists" (Genovese, 232). The majority of whites in the South were Baptists. Slave owners who allowed their slaves to practice religion naturally desired they practice that religion of their owners.

SUMMARY

By the time of the Civil War, all-black churches existed in nearly all of the Southern States. Most black church members were Baptists, prompting someone to say, "If you see a Negro who is not a Baptist or Methodist, some White man has been tampering with his religion." They were primarily Baptist because:

(1) Christ drew them to Himself through the gospel preached by Baptist ministers

(2) The fervent evangelism of the Baptist revivalists and preachers

(3) The preachers themselves and their style of preaching

(4) The emotionalism of the Baptist (and Methodist) preachers

(5) The autonomy of Baptist church polity

(6) The ease with which men were licensed and ordained

(7) The leveling quality or egalitarianism (equalizing) of the Gospel

(8) The ability of the slaves to blend what they learned and make it their own

(9) And the overall thrust, the all-pervading influence of slavery and racism.

These all worked together, mixed and meshed, creating spiritual, religious, psychological, educational, physical, social, and economic reasons why the blacks became Baptists in such predominant numbers. The God of the Bible is no respecter of persons, faces or races, but One Who uses us where He finds us. He takes all things, fulfills His purpose, and makes them work out for the good of those He calls.

Notes

1. James H. Satterfield, "The Baptists and the Negro Prior to 1863," unpublished Ph.D. dissertation, Southern Baptist Theological Seminary (1919), 96. W.E. Du Bois, *The Souls of Black Folk*, 198. M. J. Herskovits, 232-235. Wesley M. Gewehr, 106. Milton C. Sernett, *Black Religion*, 84.

2. William H. Pipes, *Say Amen Brother!* , 169, fn 13. Curtis D. Duncan, "A Historical Survey of the Development of the Black Baptist Church in the U.S. and a Study of Performance Practices Associated with D. Watts Hymn Singing: A Source Book for Teachers." Ed.D. dissertation, Washington University, 1979 (Michigan; University Micro-films International, 1979) 97: "Most singing of the slaves was influenced by the African heritage. Examples of call and response singing, intricate syncopation, and surging lines, rhythm, body movement and repetition all point to African survivals in Black song." See also Brackney, 106.

3. Berlin, 69. Miles Mark Fisher, *A Short History*, 91. John W. Blassingame, ed. *Slave Testimony*, 218: see the interview with the slave, Madison Jefferson.

CHAPTER 5

TIMES OF ADVERSITY

The American Colonization Society

Several things occurred in the last period, 1776-1820, that claim our attention now. One is the formation in 1816-1817 of the American Colonization Society, under the leadership of the Presbyterian minister, Robert S. Finley[1]. The primary aim of colonization, with Congressional approval, was to remove the free blacks, and those who would become free in a territory, and send them back to Africa (Wright, 265; Handy, 186). Approximately 12,000 slaves actually were colonized and went to the continent, primarily to Liberia. Up to 1852, some 7,836 blacks had been sent to Africa.[2]

The sources of free blacks include those freed (1) whose terms expired as indentured servants (2) after the owner's death by will (3) by the owners who protested the slave system (4) because of crop failure (5) because of family ties with the whites, as was sometimes the case with mulattoes (6) Children born of free blacks and children born of free blacks and Indians (7) those who would become free in a territory. There were about one and a half million blacks in the U.S. in 1816, of which approximately thirteen percent were free (Wright, 262). The goals of the Colonization Society created little enthusiasm among the blacks.

Southern blacks objected to colonization but not in the same manner as did the Northern blacks (Staudenraus, 188; Sobel, 226). It is said that a white missionary offered a black slave an opportunity to return to Africa. The slave replied, "I crossed the ocean once, but I made up my mind then never to trust myself in a boat with a white man again" (Park, 118). Hard-to-kill rumors spread that those blacks who went to Africa were mistreated, or soon after arriving, became diseased and died. Free blacks then were never enthusiastic about the Society (Fisher, 62; Williams, 125).

Blacks considered colonization a scheme to re-enslave them. Generally, black preachers opposed the movement (Woodson, *History* 170). In time, some black leaders began to advocate colonization in some country other than those in Africa. In Philadelphia, leaders of the black community made it known that America was their true home.[3] "We will never separate ourselves voluntarily from the slave population of this country." They would fight colonization even down to their deaths (Staudenraus, 32; Mehlinger, 283).

Despite the pressure put on free blacks to leave, the effort failed. Told they would never attain equality here, and would remain in an inferior position—a black man in a white man's country taken from the red man—the blacks resisted colonization. By 1830, the managers of the Society knew that the entire concept of colonization created only antagonism and resistance among the majority of the free blacks.

Among the freedmen, Frederick Douglass was considered the Society's greatest enemy (Mehlinger, 295). Among the whites, William Lloyd Garrison, 1805-1879, abolitionist leader, editor and lecturer, bitterly assailed the motives and behavior of those who favored or advocated colonization. To Garrison their motives were not only mistaken, but evil. He wrote ten reasons why he opposed colonization: (1) it is not a pledge to out and out oppose the cruel practice of slavery. Rather, colonization shields slavery from direct attack.

(2) It apologizes for slavery and the slave holders (3) recognizes slaves as property (4) colonization would increase the value of slaves (5) colonization is the enemy of immediate abolition (6) the movement feeds on fear, selfishness, and racial prejudice. (7) Its goal is the complete expulsion of free blacks (8) free blacks are disparaged, slandered, terrorized (9) the colonization movement denies the possibility of blacks being elevated in the U.S., thus obstructing black advancement, blinds them to the impracticality of removing the entire black population (10) and the colonization movement deceives and misleads the country (Wright, 261-317).

YEAR[4]	SLAVES	FREE	TOTAL SLAVES (All States)	TOTAL FREE (All States)	TOTAL BLACK POP.
1790	697,697	59,481			757,178 (Jones, 5)
1800	Va.-345,796 S.C.-146,151 N.C.-133,296	Va.-20,124 Md.-19,587 Pa.-14,564	893,041	108,398 110,555 (Jones, 62)	1,001,439 1,003,569 (Jones, 62)
1810	Va.-392,518 S.C.-196,365 N.C.-168,824	Md.-33,927 Va.-30,570 N.Y.-25,333	1,191,364	186,446 195,643 (Jones, 62)	1,377,810 1,387,007 (Jones, 62)
1820	Va.-425,153 S.C.-258,475 N.C.-205,017	Md.-39,730 Va.-36,889 Pa.-30,202 N.Y.-29,279	1,543,688 1,538,064 (Jones, 62)	233,566 244,020 (Jones, 62)	1,777,254 1,782,084 (Jones, 62)
1830	Va.-469,757 S.C.-315,401 N.C.-245,601	Md.-52,938 Va.-47,348 N.Y.-44,870 Pa.-37,930	2,009,043	319,599	2,328,642
1840			2,487,113	386,235	2,873,348 (Jones, 100)
1860			3,953,760	448,070	4,441,830[5]

Marriage among the Slaves

After the 1830s, the situation for black Baptists (and Methodists) became worse, especially in the South where most of the blacks lived. Even though the law was passed in 1808 forbidding the importation of any more slaves, it was poorly enforced. Slaves still were imported secretly into the U.S. until 1862 (Park, 116). The lot of the slave did not improve. Probably the worst aspect of slave social life was the denial of the legal right to marry. Adultery, concubinage, fornication, infidelity, desertion—all such have demoralizing effects upon any society. Where legal marriage is not sanctioned because the participants have no legal rights, immorality will have a field day. The union between male and female slaves was at best just a temporary arrangement. Slaves simply were not entitled to the privilege of matrimony (Tyms, 30). Henry Bibb, a slave, said:

> Marriage among American slaves is disregarded by the laws of this country. It is counted a mere temporary matter; it is a union which may be continued or broken off, with or without the consent of a slaveholder, whether he is a priest or a libertine (Bayliss, 95).

Betsy Crissman, a slave, was interviewed and stated, "I was married in East Tennessee and lived with my husband six years. Then his master took him to Alabama, and I never saw him any more." Another slave, Lewis Hayden, was of the opinion that white ministers and professors of religion saw separating slave families a thing no more evil than separating a litter of pigs or selling any domestic animal (Blassingame, 468, 696f). Is it any wonder someone stated, "There must be a Hell, for if not, where will slave masters go?" On the other hand, Gutman suggests family life among the slaves was better than whites make out it was.

He estimates that only one in six (or seven) slave marriages actually ended by force or sale (Sobel, 173). He believes that whites simply did not see the black family structure, even as they did not see the black church, the *invisible institution* that existed on the plantations; the black family too was invisible. Nevertheless, while not legally wed, they lived as mates and other slaves recognized them as such. One breath of fresh air in this matter was the attempt of Andrew Bryan to strengthen the marital relations of church members (Simms, 44). He was a slave, born in 1737 at Goose Creek, South Carolina, and converted under the preaching of George Leile, mentioned earlier in connection with the Silver Bluff Church. Bryan was a remarkable man, instrumental in constituting the African Baptist Church in Savannah in 1788.

He required candidates for baptism to give full proof of their marriage relationship. If they lived together as was commonly done without benefit of marriage, Bryan made them come to him and have a wedding ceremony performed. Those intending to get married were to make it known to the deacons on the plantation, or to the pastor in the city. What boldness of this black Baptist preacher of more than two hundred years ago, who without help from the State, sought to lift up the standards of conjugality in a slave society!

Some whites believed God cursed blacks, according to their interpretation of Genesis 9:25. They saw in the status quo divine sanction. Furthermore, many whites considered slavery a political issue, not a moral one (Scherer, 144; Banks, *Slavery* 116). Such a mentality made it easy to justify further disfranchisement of free blacks, and suppression of voices crying for the abolition of slavery. Attempts were made also to control black churches by withholding ordination of black preachers.

Rebellions

One of the things that profoundly affected the black church was rebellion. Slave rebellions became a major cause of the limitations imposed upon the blacks by the whites during this period. "The more alarming insurrections of the first quarter of the nineteenth century were the immediate cause of the most reactionary measures." There were 47 known slave revolts between 1741 and 1800. There occurred approximately 210 revolts between 1791 and 1856.[6]

The three outstanding rebellions were those of (1) Gabriel Prosser, c. 1775-1800. His plan was to seize Richmond, Virginia, kill off most of the whites and eventually make Virginia a State for blacks. An attack was planned in August, 1800, but was postponed because of a flood. Two slaves told their owners of the plot, and Prosser along with about 34 of his 1,000 followers were captured and hanged.

(2) Denmark Vesey, c. 1767-1822, in 1822 plotted in Charleston, South Carolina, to attack several cities. His planned revolt involved about 9,000 free blacks and slaves, more than in any other uprising in American history. Informed on by other slaves, Vesey was captured. He and about 35 of his followers were hanged.

(3) Nat Turner's rebellion in 1831 took place in Southampton County, Virginia. Some 61 whites were killed; and the whites killed more than 100 blacks. Turner's revolt "gave the South a jolt by which it would never fully recover." When it was made known that Turner was a preacher, the reaction to other black preachers was disastrous. They were accused of using the pulpit to incite resurrection (Dennard, 186; Stampp, 157; Woodson, *History* 131).

Reactions to the Rebellions

The Southern white Baptists turned the spotlight on black preachers. In 1832, Virginia passed a law silencing black preachers. They could not function without the presence of a white man. Baptist autonomy made it difficult to monitor the blacks, and the whites could develop no systematic strategies to prevent blacks from preaching. Whites simply did not have the time, personnel or legal authority (for what such authority mattered) to stringently supervise black religion. John Floyd, governor of Virginia, said, "The public good requires the Negro preachers to be silenced" (Dennard, 200).

Because of Nat Turner's rebellion, whites attempted to stop the mouths of the slave preachers. They revoked more licenses to preach than they granted. However, black preachers continued heralding the Word clandestinely in their quarters.

In 1833, Alabama required five respectable slave-holders to be present and for some neighboring religious society to have given authorization before the black preacher could speak. In 1834, Georgia passed a law that no more than seven be present unless justices on the certification of three white ordained ministers licensed the black preacher. You can see how black churches became "colored branches," or wards of the white churches (Meier and Rudwick, 87). Other Southern States followed the examples of these States, passing regulations even more stringent. Some even sought to expel all free blacks from their commonwealths.

Not only was there an attempt to silence preachers and restrict assemblies, but passes became more difficult to obtain. Passes or "tickets" were required by blacks to attend church. To be found without one could lead to a beating or imprisonment. If the overseer were in the mood to grant a pass to the slave who desired to attend church, he would write, "Permit the bearer to pass and repass to _____, this evening, unmolested," and sign it (Sobel, 169; Sernett, 66). A slave, Sarah Fitzpatrick, born in 1847 in Alabama, was interviewed and said,

> In them times Negroes had to have a pass to go to church too. White folks asked you what church you wanted to go to and they issue you a pass, write on there the name of the church and the name of the person and the time to get back home. Course when Negroes went to church with their White folks they didn't have to have no pass. You see, us Negroes had our meeting in the White folks Baptist Church in the town of Tuskegee. There's a place up in the loft there now that they built for the Negro slaves to attend church with the White folks (Blassingame,

642, written in dialect).

A fourth step taken as reaction to Nat Turner's insurrection was the forbidding teaching blacks how to read or write. We do not suggest that these restrictions first occurred at this time. Rather, the rebellions moved the whites in fear to crack down. Blassingame (416f) tells of one slave born in Maryland in 1811, who said, "It was a rule in that county, that a slave must not be seen with a book of any kind; but old madam Bean, my mistress, belonged to the Baptist Church, and she said we might all learn to spell and read the Bible."

Obviously, this restriction meant that Southern Blacks could no longer use the church as an institution of secular education (Woodson, *Education* 184f). By 1834, the Sunday Schools, which had been greatly used to teach blacks to read and write, were forced to give only oral instruction. By 1840, only fifteen Sunday Schools in the South existed, with an attendance of about 1,459. It is neither the number of revolts nor the extent of the revolts that is significant according to Genovese (588). What is important is that the insurrections provided a measurement of the degree of the resentment within the hearts of an enslaved people. Rebellions represent the "ultimate manifestation of class war under the most unfavorable conditions."

All of the scholars consulted for this work agree that the drastic restrictions placed upon the blacks during this period were essentially ineffective! Taking away what religious freedom the blacks had up to the time of Turner's rebellion, proved a fruitless proscription; it did not prevent them from performing their mission. In spite of all opposition, the ingenuity, sense of purpose, and determination of the preachers enabled them to succeed (Dennard, 250, 255). Despite the restrictions and supervision of the whites, the black church survived. Measures taken to limit the blacks were futile and ineffectual.

It bears repeating: Attitudes and relationships between blacks and whites during the period between 1821 and 1865 became increasingly poor. Gradually the blacks lost their voting rights as Baptists in mixed church business meetings. Whites stopped calling them "Brother" and "Sister," titles that were not only biblical, but had symbolic social significance, implication and importance as well. As the numbers of blacks increased in the general population, naturally their numbers increased in the church. More and more the question asked by the whites was, "What shall we do with them?" (Haynes, 122). Options listed included: (1) sending all of them back to Africa (2) keep all of them in slavery, including the free blacks (3) *gradually* free all of them (4) *immediate* emancipation (5) keep the slaves, but ship the free blacks to Africa.

Now by the 1840s "whatever institutional character antislavery might have had, either as colonization or abolition, had broken down" (Elkins, 184). Whatever power national church organizations may have had to improve the lot of the slaves disappeared. Most white Baptists in the South were not great slave owners. The large plantation families of Virginia, Georgia, the Carolinas, Alabama and Mississippi were descendants, for the most part, of the colonial aristocrats, who were of the Anglican or Presbyterian denominations (Armstrong & Armstrong, 164).

In time, however, the abolition movement increased its intensity. Baptists who owned even one family of black slaves, in general aligned themselves with the plantation owners. With increased pressure for abolition from the North—the American Missionary Association spoke out boldly against Southern slavery greed and against Northern servile acquiescence—and the South more and more in favor of slavery, it is no wonder that a break took place in the various white denominations (Beard, 13). In addition, of course, a still wider break would occur between the North and South—the Civil War!

Notes

1. Official name: American Society for the Colonization of Free People of Color: Sandy D. Martin, "Black Baptists," 65. *Black Americans and the Missionary Movement in Africa*, (edited by Sylvia M. Jacobs).

2. Louis R. Mehlinger, "The Attitude of the Free Negro toward African Colonization," 301: From 1820 to 1833, some 2,885 blacks went, most of them freed *in order to* go to Africa. The 7,836 that emigrated up to 1852 are broken down as follows: 2,720 were born free; 204 purchased their freedom; owners manumitted 3,868 to emigrate; and the government liberated 1,044 Africans.

3. The annual convention of the Free Colored People was first held here in Philadelphia (Mehlinger, 290).

4. These figures are taken from "A Statistical View of the population of the U.S.," 1790-1830, published by the Department of State in 1835; and from the "Statistical Abstract of the U.S.," 1898, published by the U.S. Government in 1899: Cited by Leonard L. Haynes, *The Negro Community within American Protestantism, 1619-1844,* 85-88. Charles C. Jones, *The Religious Instruction of the Negro in the U. S.*, 5 62, 100. For the statistics on Slaves and Free, only the three (or four) leading States were culled out of the twenty-eight, including Washington, D. C., mentioned for each decade.

5. WBE, "Black Americans," "By 1860, about 4 million slaves lived in the South ... about 490,000 free blacks."

6. The industrial revolution also made Southern whites more aware of the threat an enlightened black populace would be: Carter G. Woodson, *Education,* 152, 155.

CHAPTER 6

PREACHERS AND CHURCHES

John Jasper

During this period, one outstanding black Baptist preacher was John Jasper, born in Fluvana County, Virginia, July 4, 1812, and died in 1901. Converted at the age of 27 while working in a tobacco warehouse, he felt the compulsion to preach, and shared his conversion experiences with all whom he met, white or black, overseer or slave. An illiterate man, he started to learn to read with the aid of a New York speller and with the Bible, a book many slaves used to learn to read.[1] The slaves held the Bible in high esteem.

Stories of redemption were especially treasured: Joseph from a pit to Potiphar's place to a prison to Pharaoh's palace; Israel from slavery in the land of Egypt to the Promised Land; the crumbling walls of Jericho; David's defeat of Goliath; the three Hebrews delivered from the fiery furnace; and Daniel freed from the lions' den.

These stories, along with the miracles of Christ, His death, burial and resurrection, freedom in Christ, His second coming—were outstanding in the hearts and minds of the slaves (Brackney, 106). The Bible helped them to survive. Although white missionaries and evangelists brought the Bible to the blacks, and other whites lived contradictory to its teachings, the blacks sensed there was something special, something supernatural about the Scriptures.

Jasper preached the Bible. He had an excellent memory, with an ability to put in words what his mind so vividly imagined. Coupled with his common sense approach and practical experiences, he demonstrated his good grasp of the Bible in such a way that he became an outstanding preacher, popular with the whites as well as with his own people. If one defines "old fashioned" or "old time" preaching as the emotional preaching of uneducated black ministers (originally of slavery days), then Jasper's preaching summarized all

57

such black preaching (Pipes, 65, 163 fn 3). This is not to suggest that the less emotional, more intellectual type of preaching did not exist in some black churches during slavery time. Noted also as one of the best examples of the late antebellum funeral orators, Jasper built quite a reputation in the Richmond-Petersburg area as a funeral preacher (Sobel, 199). He founded the Sixth Mount Zion Baptist Church, and pastored there in Richmond until death sealed his lips.

Preachers: Black and White

All too often, the southern white preachers used the pulpit to maintain the status quo. The slave John Anderson related he never heard any ministers denouncing slavery, and said that any who dared do so would not be allowed to preach. Another slave, George Ross, felt that the religious feeling was used to induce slaves to imagine they owed a duty to their owners more than to God (Blassingame, 353, 407).

Howard Thurman's grandmother, who had been a slave in the northern part of the State of Florida, told him how the slave owner would have the white minister come to hold religious services for the slaves. She said the minister would always preach from the same text, "Slaves, be obedient to your masters, for this is right in the Lord."[2] She also told Thurman about the slave preacher permitted from time to time to preach to them (and to the slaves from neighboring plantations as well). No matter where he began in the Bible, he always ended up at Calvary (Goodwin, 533). Would to God the same could be said today!

Genovese (716, fn 24) notes that white preachers "varied their texts a good deal, and often did deliver messages of spiritual equality before God. But they could not avoid the theme of submission to slavery, and they thereby often ruined good efforts." As the number of blacks attending increased, they tended to dominate the meeting with their religious fervor—whether in singing, testifying, shouting, etc. (Sobel, 210). Some whites were glad to get away, or permit the blacks to have their own separate churches and church business meetings—with white supervision. Important decisions from such meetings had to be submitted to the whites for approval. See this period as one in which the whites became less and less willing to share their church life with the blacks; and the blacks increasingly desiring independence to worship as they pleased. From "the 1830s until the Civil War . . . the existence of Negro churches in the South was at the whim of local white authorities. Any independence was strictly nominal" (Sernett, 114f).

Growth of the Churches

Despite adversity black Baptist churches grew. White and black missionaries from the North helped the slave and free blacks in the South. Blacks experienced tremendous growth as they surged to build their own independent churches and to build up their own denomination. In the North during the antebellum period, the development of black Baptists did not proceed as smoothly as might be expected. However, they continued to grow. Though many had their own churches in the North, they usually belonged to white associations; and the blacks used the whites' literature, a cause of disagreement in later years; and they imbibed their doctrines.

In the South, the insurrections stymied black Methodism more so than they did black Baptists. However, in the North, Methodism was stronger among the blacks. In the West growth was tremendous. Fugitive slaves and freed blacks founded a new group of Baptist churches in the West. First, note the Early Churches: The independent black Baptist churches organized before 1845 in the South and in the North. Second, there is a list of the First Black Baptist Churches in each of twenty-six States, up to 1860. Third, there is a table showing the largest black Baptist churches, North and South, prior to the end of the Civil War. Independent black churches were much smaller numerically during the period under study.

Table I – Independent Black Baptist
Churches Organized before 1845

In the South:
1. Silver Bluff, Aiken Country, S.C., 1773-1775.
2. Harrison Street, Petersburg, Va., 1776.[3]
3. First African, Savannah, Ga., 1778.[4]
4. First Colored, Richmond, Va., 1780
5. First Colored, Williamsburg, Va, 1785[5]
6. First Colored, Lexington, Ky, 1790
7. Springfield, Augusta, Ga., 1793.[6]
8. Portsmouth, Va., 1798
9. Second African, Savannah, Ga., 1802[7]
10. Gillfield Baptist, Petersburg, Va., 1803[8]
11. Stone Street, Mobile, Ala., 1806
12. African, Claiborne County, Miss., 1809
13. Calvary Baptist, Bayou Chicot, La., 1812
14. African, Pike County, Miss., 1820
15. Fifth Street, Louisville, Ky., 1820[9]
16. First Baptist, (Colored), St. Louis, Mo., 1822[10]
17. First African, New Orleans, Louisana, 1826
18. First Baptist, (Colored), Washington, DC, 1832
19. First Baptist, (Colored), Baltimore, Md., 1836
20. First Baptist (Colored), Jacksonville, Fla., 1838
21. Nineteenth St. Bapt. (Colored), Washington, D.C., 1839

In the North:[11]
1. African Baptist, Boston, Mass., 1805[12]
2. Abyssinian, New York City, 1808[13]
3. First African (Cherry Street), Phila., Pa., 1809[14]
4. First Colored, Trenton, N. J., 1812.
   Salem or Wood River Baptist, Illinois, 1812?
5. The Ebenezer, N. Y. C., N. Y., 1825
6. Union Baptist, Cincinnati, Ohio, 1827
7. First Baptist, St. Louis, Mo., 1827[15]
8. Union Baptist, Phila., Pa., 1832
9. First Baptist, Baltimore, Md., 1836
10. Shiloh Baptist, Phila., Pa., 1842

Table II – The First Black Baptist
Church in Each State [16]

1. South Carolina, Aiken County: Silver Bluff, 1773-1775
2. Virginia, Williamsburg: 1776 [17]
3. Georgia, Savannah: First African, 1778
4. Kentucky, Lexington: 1790 (constituted c. 1786)
5. Massachusetts, Boston: African or Joy Street, 1805
6. Alabama, Mobile: Stone Street, 1806
7. New York, New York City, Abyssinian, 1808
8. Pennsylvania, Philadelphia: First African, 1809
9. Mississippi, Claiborne County: 1809 [18]
10. Louisiana, Bayou Chicot: Calvary Church, 1812
11. New Jersey, Trenton: First Colored, 1812
12. Illinois, Wood River: Salem or Wood River, 1819 [19]
13. Missouri, St. Louis: First African, 1822 [20]
14. Ohio, Cincinnati: Union Colored, 1827
15. North Carolina, Rowan and Davidson Counties: Five churches constituted about 1830-1831
16. Florida, Deland: St. Anne Primitive Baptist, 1832 (?)
17. Maryland, Baltimore: First Colored, 1836
18. Connecticut, Hartford: Colored Branch of the First Baptist Church [21]
19. Washington, D. C.: First Colored, 1839
20. Rhode Island, Providence: Meeting Street Church, 1840
21. Tennessee, Columbia: Mt. Lebanon Bapt. Church, 1843
22. Arkansas, Pine Bluff: First Baptist, 1853
23. Texas, Matagorda County: Colored Bapt. Church, 1854
24. Michigan, Detroit: Groghan Street Baptist, 1855
25. Kansas, Leavenworth: Leavenworth Baptist, 1858
26. Wisconsin, Racine: Racine Baptist Church, 1860

Table III – The Largest Black Baptist Churches, North and South [22]

North: Name	Year	Membership
African, Boston, Mass.	1851	110
Abyssinian, N. Y. City	1860	440
Ebenezer, N. Y. City	1855	108
Zion, N. Y. City	1851	378
First African, Phila., Pa.	1859	268
Shiloh, Phila., Pa.	1859	303
Union, Phila., Pa.	1859	359
Chillicothe, Chillicothe, Ohio	1845	181
	Total:	2,144

South: Name	Year	Membership
First African, Petersburg, Va.	1851	1635
Gillfield, Petersburg, Va.	1851	1361
First African, Richmond, Va.	1859	3160
Second African, Richmond, Va.	1859	1029
Springfield, Augusta, Ga.	1863	1711
First African, Savannah, Ga.	1862	1815
Second Colored, Savannah, Ga.	1862	1146
First African, Lexington, Ky.	1861	2223
	Total:	14,080

Notes

1. Wm. J. Simmons, *Men of Mark*, 1064-72. See also Wm. E. Hatcher, *John Jasper: The Unmatched Black Philosopher and Preacher*. Harrison, Va.: Sprinkle Publications, 1985; and Richard E. Day, *Rhapsody in Black: the Life Story of John Jasper*. Valley Forge: Judson Press, 1967.

2. Ephesians 6:5; Colossians 3:22; Titus 2:9; I Peter 2:18.

3. Lewis G. Jordan, *Negro Baptist History, U. S. A., 1750-1930*, 25. Albert J. Raboteau, *Slave Religion*, 137: "before White Baptists did so." Owen D. Pelt and Ralph L. Smith, *Story of the National Baptists*, 37: before 1780.

4. James D. Tyms, *Rise of Religious Education among Negro Baptists*, 110: This church was begun about 1785, organized 1788. Cf. Carter G. Woodson *The History of the Negro Church*, 85.

5. Founded *by* whites *for* blacks.

6. Pelt and Smith, 46 give 1795 as the year.

7. Tyms, 111: gives the year, 1803.

8. Jackson, 22.

9. Jordan, 25, gives the year, 1829; cf. Jackson, 22.

10. Jordan, 25, the year, 1823.

11. "There is absolutely no trace of Negro Baptist churches in the North prior to the nineteenth century," Walter H. Brooks, "Priority," 172.

12. Sernett, 120, "later known as the Joy Street Church"; Jordan, 25; according to Pelt and Smith, 48, the year 1804.

13. Tyms, 111: the year, 1803; Sernett, 120: probably in 1809; Jordan, *Up the Ladder,* 183f.

14. May 14, 1808, with 13 people: Litwack, 195.

15. Tyms, 111; Jackson, 22, the year: 1823.

16. Minutes of various associations may yet be discovered that will change these "firsts," but as best ascertained from Sobel and others, these are the *first* Black Baptist churches constituted up to 1860 in the States mentioned.

17. Established *for* blacks *by* local white congregation, Pelt and Smith, 37.

18. According to fragmentary records. In Bayou Pierre, an African church is mentioned in the minutes of 1810.

19. There is no record of the constitution or affiliation.

20. Sobel, 235, gives 1827 date constituted.

21. Black members met separately.

22. Prior to 1865; Sobel, 215

CHAPTER 7

RECONSTRUCTION AND EDUCATION

Reconstruction: 1865 - 1877

The period from the end of the Civil War in 1865 to 1877, the Reconstruction era, is one of the most controversial times in the history of America. In many ways, it "far surpassed the atrocities of slavery" (Hurst, 41). Following the War there was tremendous upheaval. The conflict left the Southland decimated; its railroad system and factories destroyed. Most southern whites did not, would not accept the freed blacks as equals. And the "basic reason for White opposition to the Reconstruction governments was that most Southern Whites could not accept the idea of former slaves voting and holding office" (WBE, "Reconstruction").

Deep sectional and racial hatred appeared. Desolation, disease, loss of property, loss of jobs, combined to increase white rage, especially against black religion and political leaders (Fitts, 234). Freed men were illiterate: Seventy percent of the southern blacks in 1880 still could not read or write. Various State governments calculated to disenfranchise, intimidate and terrorize passed Black Codes. Lynching and violence succeeded in keeping blacks from voting. The Ku Klux Klan founded at Pulaski, Tennessee, in 1866 was just one of many other secret white supremacy groups.

The weak and unstable coalition called the Republican Party in the South was composed of a small number of *carpetbaggers* (Northern whites, many of whom were former Union soldiers), and *scalawags* (Southern whites), and black freedmen. Greatly fearing the population explosion of the blacks, whites sought ways to check their numerical growth. Bruce (260f) contends that it was necessary for the preservation of a stable American government to disfranchise the blacks partially.

Meanwhile, up North, there were similar attitudes expressed. In the South, church groups that had preached the Good News to the blacks ceased their activities after the War (Weatherford, 248). As relationships between former black slaves and former white masters became extremely bitter during this period, so relationships of former freed blacks *and* newly freed blacks with the whites worsened. Many northern whites were openly hostile to the aspirations of the freedmen. Whites exhibited only a superficial commitment to the egalitarian thrust of Reconstruction.

However, the black churches flourished! The loss of interest in the welfare of the blacks on the part of the whites was a challenge. The increased hostility served to strengthen the black churches and to infuse them with new life. Through new assemblies founded on the initiative of individuals or groups—through splits and schisms, missions of other churches—black churches increased greatly in numbers (Mays and Nicholson, 29).

After the Emancipation Proclamation became effective January 1, 1863, blacks moved in great numbers to organize their own assemblies; whites made no efforts to deter them (Smith, 226). When 38 blacks belonging to the white Fairfield Baptist Church decided to form their own Shiloh Baptist Church, Northumberland County, Virginia, they addressed the following petition to the white brethren on July 7, 1867:

To Elder William Kirk and the Members of the Fairfield Baptist Church:

Beloved Brothers, Grace be unto you and peace from God, the father of our Lord Jesus Christ. From an earnest desire to act in all things with an eye single to the glory of God and for the unity of that common faith which constitute us in Christ Jesus, we have thought it advisable to counsel on the subject of our future church relation.

So that whatever may be done we may at least preserve that peace and harmony which ought to characterize those of the same faith and order and promote the prosperity of that cause which, through your instrumentality, had been the means of calling us into the light and knowledge of the glorious gospel of the Son of God.

Without alluding to the Providence that so mysteriously changed our social and political relation, we conceive that under the new order of things we are not only advanced in our religious privilege, but that solemn and weighty responsibilities impose upon us a new class of duties in which we should be wanting in fidelity if we did not seek to place ourselves in that position in which we could best promote our mutual good, both in reference to ourselves and our posterity.

In this new relation the subject of a separate church organization presses itself upon us as the best possible way in which we can best promote those indispensable interests, such as an ordained ministry, a separate congregation with all the privileges of a church organization, stated church meetings, regular religious service, Sabbath schools, etc.

But just at this point the question arises: Can we not do this and preserve the unity of the faith and continue in church fellowship with our white brethren: and thereby perpetuate our church identity, so that in all the general interest of the church we may be mutually interested and to some extent co-laborers? To effect this may require the concurrent action of all the members of the congregation concerned, and the object of this communication is to ask your attention to this subject with the hope that such an arrangement can be made as to induce a general church meeting at some convenient time and place for this purpose, that our identity may be preserved or perpetuated if possible, and if not, that we may receive your parting benediction and blessing, as well as your endonation [endorsement] of our Christian character and standing. All of which is most respectfully submitted for your prayerful consideration and action. Hoping that unerring wisdom may guide us in the way of all truth, we remain, dear brethren in the bonds of Christ.

Yours Fraternally,
Samuel Conway, Secretary
Hirman Kenner, Chairman

On August 10, 1867, the members of the congregation in their regular church business meeting read and accepted the letter.[1] They granted the petition by unanimous vote. Two members gave the blacks small parcels of land on which to build a temporary place of worship. In this period we see the invisible institution which had existed in slavery, known and unknown to whites, but all limited in their autonomy—merge with the visible churches of the blacks who had been free before the Civil War.

Vigorously entering upon their newfound freedom, the black churches experienced enormous growth. "White racism was probably the greatest single factor in moving black people to establish churches of their own." White churches were almost emptied of blacks, who left to (1) symbolically express their new freedom (2) show they could maintain their own churches (3) make God's house a house of opportunity for *all* people (Smith, 228).

No more special pews to remind the blacks of an imposed social inferiority. No more exhorting them to be good slaves. No more white preachers speaking over their heads. No more feeling ill at ease, straitjacketed, unable to worship, shout, sing, pray, moan, and preach as they pleased.

No more white supervision! For as Bruce (107) adds, "The colored pastors [who] are very jealous of their prerogative." Black reaction to adversities gave rise to cooperative movements in the forms of association, State and National conventions, black schools and the black press (Fitts, 241). Within the black Baptist churches could be found all kinds of activities which enabled them to face the rigors of the times. They developed their Sunday Schools, created all kinds of mutual aid societies, insurance societies, women's groups, secret societies, and mass meetings; they performed skits and plays, gave recitals, held debates, sold suppers, sponsored lectures, etc. (Du Bois, 143).

The Reconstruction era ended with the Compromise of 1877. Southern Democrats in Congress agreed not to oppose the decision of the Electoral Commission that had a Republican majority, if the Republicans agreed to end Reconstruction and pull out federal troops from the South. As a result, Rutherford B. Hayes became President, and promptly did as he promised. Reconstruction served to consolidate the black church and make it even more the very hub of black American society.

The American Baptist Home Mission Society

Augustus F. Beard (147) said,

> No race can be permanently dependent upon another race for its ultimate development. This Negro race must be taught to save itself and how to do it; to work out its own future with its own teachers and educators. Therefore, reliance must be placed on permanent institutions and permanent teachers for them, and for the steady and determined consecration of those ready to take up the work with this high conception of it.

What Beard said remains true; the record bears witness of the outstanding work of the American Baptist Home

Mission Society (ABHMS), formed April 27, 1832, to "promote the preaching of the Gospel in North America" (Fisher, 48). By 1870, this group had established or helped to found twenty-one schools for the freedmen.

Earlier, 1832-1862, the ABHMS did very little among American blacks. This was a very tense period in America so far as race relations were concerned. Only later, as Emancipation approached, did the Society take steps to help educate the freedmen (Torbet, 378). In the years immediately following the Civil War, northern white Baptists made deep inroads among the black Baptists of the South, especially in their work in higher education (Reid, 19).

The southern white Baptists abandoned the blacks, possibly because the old relationship of master and slave no longer obtained, and they could not dictate church policy or spiritual development. However, the northern white Baptists moved in to help an illiterate people greatly in need of aid. They came with their trained missionaries, administrators, teachers, and with finances, to work not only with black children, but also with black preachers. In fact, training of ministers was the early purpose of the Society (White, 102-113). One strong point of the ABHMS was its willingness to cooperate with independent black groups to contribute to the support of the schools founded.

Black churches, associations, and conventions contrib.-uted some funds and moral support (Meir and Rudwick, 163; Fitts 178). The northern whites established new churches, published Christian Education literature, and set up education facilities throughout the South. From 1865-1905 there was the tremendous period in the development of education among black Baptists; indeed, the majority of the schools founded by whites for blacks came into existence before 1888 (Tyms, 133). The Congregational Denomination (in principle, the American Missionary Association was undenominational, but depended primarily on the Congregationalists) established during this period the following schools: Hampton Institute, 1868, Hampton, Virginia; Howard University, 1867, Washington, D. C.; Fisk

University, 1865, Nashville, Tennessee; and Atlanta University, 1865, Atlanta, Georgia (Latourette, 1252).

Educational Efforts of the Blacks

In the years immediately following the Civil War, blacks depended largely on public schools and those set up for the Freedmen's Bureau. After the Reconstruction period, blacks made greater strides developing their own secondary schools in churches, log cabins, and abandoned buildings (Fitts, 179). Booker T. Washington, Baptist layman, was born a slave in Virginia, in 1856, but became the most influential black leader and educator of his day. He graduated from Hampton Institute, and then founded the Tuskegee Normal and Industrial Institute, Tuskegee, Alabama, in 1881. Washington served as principal and instructor for 33 years.

By the year 1900, black Baptist associations supported some 80 elementary schools and 18 academies and colleges (L. N. Jones, 434). The AME (African Methodist Episcopal) had 32 secondary schools and colleges; the AMEZ (African Methodist Episcopal Zion), eight; and the CME (Christian— originally Colored—Methodist Episcopal), only thirty years old in 1900, had five schools.

Interracial Cooperation

During this period of educational activity, the spirit of independence increased among the black Baptists to the point that they continued to frown upon cooperation with the whites. Blacks began to feel the whites dominated black Baptist efforts in Christian Education, and that they limited the higher education goals of the blacks. Some felt such domination tended to keep blacks educationally inferior. President L. K. Williams (NBCUSA, Inc.) felt that a race of people lately emancipated needed to make friends of Christian whites if the race intended to make decent progress in life. He said,

71

Differences of opinions that led to the abortion of the founding of the Negro institutes . . . or to delay in the founding of . . . are but grains of dust that temporarily marred the relations of Negro Baptists and their sympathetic white brethren (Horace, 72).

Three schools in Texas owned and operated by black Baptists were Hearne Academy, located in Hearne, Texas; Houston Academy, in Houston; and the Guadalupe College, in Sequin, Texas. In dire straits financially, they appealed for help from ABHMS, an organization that founded Bishop College at Marshall, Texas. The Society decided it would help all three institutions if they would accept "academy" status and not seek to compete with Bishop College, but rather feed students into Bishop. From this decision came the fear that the whites sought to limit higher education aspirations of blacks, and that the purpose of the ABHMS was to keep down the blacks. The ministers split over the issue, caused a schism in the Baptist Missionary and Educational Convention that met in Calvert, Texas, in 1894. Latourette (1253) said,

The advance made by Negroes in the first half century after emancipation was phenomenal. It left much to be achieved, but when it is remembered from what a low level it began and what had been accomplished in a little over a generation for a body of people who by 1914 numbered about ten millions, the record is amazing.

To no small degree, it was due to the fact that the Negroes were immersed in the white man's culture and because many whites gave themselves unselfishly to the freedmen and their children. Much must be ascribed to the native ability of the Negroes themselves. Not a little, however, was because of the impulse which came through Christianity.

TABLES OF SCHOOLS

Name of School	Location	Year Founded or Inc.	History
Arkadelphia Academy	Arkadel-phia, KS	1890	Arkadelphia Indus-trial College; name Changed, 1892
Arkansas Baptist College	Little Rock, AK	1884	Originated by black Baptists of the State. Aided by the Society
Augusta Institute	Augusta, GA	1869	ABHMS[2]
Benedict College	Columbia, SC	1870	ABHMS; formerly Benedict Institute
Bible & Normal Institute	Memphis TN	1887	Received aid. Listed as Howe Normal & Bible Institute
Bishop College	Marshall, TX	1881	ABHMS; cooperative efforts of white Baptists, North and South, and black Baptist Associ-ates in Texas.
Central City College	Macon, GA	1899	
Central Texas Coll.	Waco, TX	1901	
Coleman Academy	Gibsland, LA	1887	
Conroe Normal & Industrial College	Conroe, TX	1903	
East Texas Normal & Industrial College	Tyler, TX	1905	Became Butler College, 1924
Florida Baptist Academy	Jacksonville, FL	1892	Received aid
Florida Institute	Live Oak, FL	1873	ABHMS; Live Oak Institute, opened, 1880. Became Florida Normal & Industrial College, St. Augustine, FL, 1892
Friendship Baptist College	Rock Hill, SC	1891	Junior College
Guadalupe College	Sequin, TX	1884	First independent black Baptist school, origin-ally at Guadalupe, TX

Name of School	Location	Year Founded or Inc.	History
Hartshorn Memmorial College	Richmond, VA	1884	See Virginia Union University
Hearne Academy	Hearne, TX	No date	
Houston Academy	Houston, TX	1885	Received aid
Howe Institute	New Iberia, LA	1888	
Jackson College	Jackson, MS	1883	1882? ABHMS. First called Natchez Seminary at Natchez, MS, 1877
Jeruel Academy	Athens, GA	No date	
Leland College	Baker, LA	1870	ABHMS, Baptist Free Missionary Society. Founded as Leland University, New Orleans, LA, 1865 (?)
Mather Industrial School	Beaufort, SC	1867	Maintained by the Women's ABHMS
Meridian Baptist Seminary	Meridian, MS	1897	
Morehouse College	Atlanta, GA	1867	ABHMS. Founded as August Institute
Morris College	Sumter, SC	1905	
Richmond Theological Institute	Richmond, VA	1876	ABHMS. First known as Colver Institute, 1867 or 1867. See Virginia Union University
Roger Williams University	Nashville, TN	1866	ABHMS. Founded as the Nashville Institute, 1866. Various dates.
Selma University	Selma, AL	1878	ABHMS, adopted 1880. Initially called Alabama Baptist Normal & Theological School, started by black Baptists
Shaw University	Raleigh, NC	1865	ABHMS. Founded as Shaw Collegiate Institute. 1865; incorporated as University, 1875

Name of School	Location	Year Founded or Inc.	History
Spelman College	Atlanta, GA	1881	ABHMS. 1882? Began as Spelman Seminary in the basement of the black Friendship Baptist. Church. Became part of Atlanta University 1929
Spiller Academy	Hampton, VA	No date	Affiliated with Virginia Union University, 1897
State University	Louisville, KY	1879	Adopted by ABHMS, 1881. Founded as Kentucky Normal & Theo-Logical Institute, renamed Simmons Univ. Closed, 1943. One of the pioneer independent black Baptist institutions of higher learning in the U.S. Founded by black Baptists of Kentucky.
Storer College	Harper's Ferry, WV	1867	Freewill Baptists. Merged with Virginia Union University, 1964
Straight University	New Orleans, LA	No date	
Talledega College	Talledega, AL	No date	
Tougalou College	Tougalou, MS	No date	
Virginia Theological Seminary & College	Lynchburg, VA	1888	Originally, Virginia Baptist Seminary, Alexandria, VA
Virginia Union University	Richmond, VA	1865	ABHMS. Wayland Coll. 1965, Washington, D.C., Consolidated, 1899, with Richmond Theol. Sem., 1876, which was first known as Colver Institute, 1867. Hartshorn merged, 1932; Storer College merged, 1964
Walker Baptist Institute	Augusta, GA	1885	Received aid

Name of School	Location	Year Founded or Inc.	History
Waters Normal Institute	Winton, NC	1887	Received aid
Wayland Seminary	Washington, DC	1865	ABHMS. 1864. Merged with Virginia Union University
Western College	Macon, MO	1890	Now located at Kansas City, Mo. Received aid

Notes

1. Taken from *Negro Church in Rural Virginia.* C. H. Hamilton and John M. Ellison. Bulletin No. 273, Virginia Agricultural Experiment Station, 1930, cited by Harry V. Richardson, *Dark Glory*, 15.

2. School established under the auspices of the American Baptist Home Mission Society. Jordan (323). Jordan gives 1867 date. Removed to Atlanta and called Atlanta Seminary, 1879; in 1897, it became Atlanta Baptist College; name changed to Morehouse College, 1912; made part of Atlanta University, 1929. Also Fitts, 161-218; A. W. Pegues, 555-617; G. F. Richings, 19-25, and C. L. White, 98-119.

CHAPTER 8

REMARKABLE GROWTH

Following Reconstruction, the blacks lost the rights they had gained. Using poll taxes, gerrymandering, grandfather clauses, etc., the whites virtually kicked the blacks out of politics. Fear too played a part, for the peak year for lynching was 1892, with 230 victims. From 1889 to 1914, approximately 2,256 blacks were lynched, mainly in the South. About 4,752 lynchings took place between 1882 and 1968. This figure includes 1,307 whites and 3,445 blacks (WBE, "Lynching").

With the political door slammed shut in their faces, the black preachers who had gotten involved in the political arena were forced to return to the church. "Some politicians who were not preachers surreptitiously got a call to preach" (Fisher, 114). This may be one reason why political methods obtained a stranglehold on black Baptist churches! Remarkable growth in their churches occurred, and the Sunday School played an important role in the development of the churches (Brunner, 87).

By 1890 there were 1,071,920 black Baptists in the U. S. (Freeman, 79). About this time, the migration of blacks began, and their relocation would have "far reaching significance to the growth and development of the Black Baptist church movement" (Fitts, 259).

Abandoning the rural areas, they flocked to the cities: From the south, they headed north, and to the west. Between 1910 and 1920, the black population increased 43.3 percent—World War I was a major contributing factor here—in the west, 55.1 percent. However, in the south, the population increased only 1.9 percent (Torbet, 415).

White Baptists: Sects, Associations, Conventions

In order to appreciate more highly the growth and development of black Baptist associations, State Conventions and National Conventions, it is necessary to look back. First, a word about white Baptists. There were all kinds of Baptists: (1) *Sixth Principle Baptists* based their faith on Hebrews 6:1-2: Repentance, faith in God, baptism, laying on of hands, the resurrection, and judgment. Laying on of hands was required after the believer was baptized. The rite became a major cause of disagreement, one more source of schism in the early years of the colonial Baptists (Brackney, 97).

(2) *Nine Principle Baptists* (3) *Particular Baptists* taught Christ died only for the elect (4) *General Baptists* believed Christ died for all who would accept Him as Savior (5) *Regular Baptists* opposed revivalism (6) *Free Will Baptists:* There is a significant group of black Free Will Baptists. Their history and beliefs follow in a later chapter.

(7) *Hard Shell Baptists* opposed missions, believing that human effort in evangelizing was sacrilegious. Winning souls was God's job, not man's; those elected will be saved without any help from man. If not elected, then no human agency under the sun could change it (Baker, 79; Throgmorton and Potter, 3-6).

(8) *Two Seed Predestinarian Baptists* believed there were two seeds in Adam's spirit. One seed was destined to Hell, the other to salvation. Everybody is born with one or the other; they cannot change. (9) *Primitive Baptists:* This group also has a large black following, and is described later. (10) *Landmarkian Baptists* proclaimed an apostolic succession through a continuous chain of true congregations from New Testament times until the present (11) *Seventh Day Baptists,* of course, are Saturday worshipers.

We stated earlier that The Philadelphia Baptist Association (PBA) is the oldest association, founded July 27, 1707. This organization wielded tremendous influence in the Colonies, and by its insistence upon conformity of both churches and preachers in doctrine and in deeds, it set the standard for all such similar associations (Boyd, 39).

The Charleston Association, South Carolina, is the second oldest, 1751; and in 1758, the Sandy Creek Association was founded in North Carolina. There was reluctance to join any association because of the fear that the autonomy of the local Baptist church would be destroyed. In time this fear was overcome. By 1790 there were thirty-four associations. By 1828 there were two hundred and nineteen, by 1836, three hundred and eighty-eight (Barnes, 14f).

In 1821, white Baptists began to form State Conventions, "and rapid progress in this direction was evidence of their desire to articulate a growing denominationalism" (Goen, 59). Reluctance to associate is understandable. In truth, a survey of the numerous Baptist bodies then in existence in the nineteenth century indicated no uniformity could be demanded or expected. The earlier Baptists in America had been greatly persecuted, and distrusting authority, wanted nothing to do with supracongregational organizations. However, the General Convention (The General Missionary Convention of the Baptist Denomination in the U. S. for Foreign Missions) formed in 1814. Meeting every three years thereafter, it became known as the Triennial Convention. The Baptist General Tract Society founded in 1824, became the American Baptist Publishing Society in the 1840s. The American Baptist Home Mission Society was organized in 1832.

Split Over Slavery

Now the main issue for the white Baptists in their first major split was slavery. Methodism had split in 1844 over this matter; and so did the Presbyterians later in 1861. In their 1844 Convention, the whites formulated this compromise:

Resolved, That, in cooperating as members of this Convention in the work of Foreign Missions, we disclaim all sanction, either express or implied, whether of slavery or of antislavery: but, as individuals, we are perfectly free both to express and to promote, elsewhere, our own views of these subjects in a Christian manner and spirit. [1]

However, there was still dissatisfaction in all camps. The delegation from the Alabama State Convention forced a showdown by asking whether a slaveholder would be accepted as a missionary if he applied for the position (Pelt and Smith, 67). The answer given:

If anyone should offer himself as a missionary, having slaves, and should insist on retaining them as his property, we could not appoint him. One thing is certain, we can never be a partner to any arrangement which would imply approbation of slavery (Barnes, 24).

At this point, the Virginia Baptist Foreign Mission Society called for interested bodies to meet at Augusta, Georgia, to consider establishing a new missionary organization. In May 1845, more than three hundred delegates from eight States and from the District of Columbia founded the Southern Baptist Convention. Thus the original white Baptist Convention lasted some thirty-one years, 1814-1845. In 1907, the Baptists in the north took the name, Northern Baptist Convention, but in 1950 changed it to the American Baptist Convention.

There were other issues involved in the 1845 split, but slavery was *the* issue. It is easy to see why there was such conflict when we realize that for twenty-one years of its existence, slaveholding presidents led the Convention (Haynes, 112). Naturally, the split greatly affected the approximately 200,000 black Baptists in the South. Church doors were slammed in their faces and conditions worsened, thus laying the groundwork for the establishment of black Baptist organizations.

Black Baptist Associations

Associations and Conventions were important in the lives of the early black Baptist churches. Although technically the Baptist associations were not much more than mutual aid societies, they gave the blacks a forum for discussion (Sobel, 129; Wheeler, 32). Mergers, name changes, dissolution, splits, faulty records, etc., all combined to make difficult tracing with accuracy the history of black Baptist Associations and Conventions (Sernett, *Black Religion* 217, n. 15).

At first black churches did not have their own associations, but sought to join whatever local white Baptist group would welcome them. Their religious experiences were interrelated with the whites in many ways, and there was too the desire for white legitimization (Tyms, 122; Sobel, 214). Thus, in the early days the blacks made no attempts to form their own associations.

During the years 1800-1830, there was no larger associational life among the separate black Baptists. Control by the white associations was strengthened by the slave codes and police laws passed in those early decades of the nineteenth century (Haynes, 143; Raboteau, 190; Sernett, *Black Religion* 114). Interestingly, the first *independent* black associations were not formed in the south or in the north, but in the Midwest States. This was probably because on the frontier there was greater need for such cooperation, and where frontier conditions prevailed there was more freedom.

Now various dates have been given for the establishment of the first black association. By the 1830s, the races had moved further apart, as far as religion was concerned, and the move for separate associations had begun. Tension between white and black Baptists increased, with the American Baptist Home Mission Society at the center of the conflict (Tyms, 113). According to the record, the Providence Missionary Baptist (District) Association (of Ohio) was organized at the Providence Baptist Church of Berlin Cross Roads, Ohio, sometime during the years 1834-1836. [2]

The Providence Missionary Baptist Association was

composed of but six Ohio churches, the largest of which had 49 members. Practically all of the original 178 members were former slaves (Sobel, 216). Its constitution stipulated the Association would not correspond with any other association that sought, directly or indirectly, to justify slavery.

The second rival association, also composed mostly of ex-slaves, was the Wood River Baptist Association of Illinois, probably organized in 1838 or 1839, though most historians support the year 1838.[3] In 1840 the New Union Association was formed and gained influence in Ohio, Indiana and Illinois. The Colored Baptist Association, Friends to Humanity, organized in 1839 in Illinois, and then split in 1849. Its northern group became the Colored Baptist Association, later changed its name, about 1856, to the Wood River Colored Baptist Association. The southern section took the name, Mount Olive Association.

In 1843, the Union Anti-Slavery Baptist Association was formed. The Providence and Wood River Associations merged in 1853 to become the Western Colored Baptist Association. [4] You see then the beginnings and growth of the Association movement. The next step is the State Convention. From the Revolutionary War until the 1830s, participation in conventions was on a local church level. Those blacks received by larger white bodies were accepted only as a black church; for years they remained tied to the white Baptist organizations (Freeman, 59; Meier and Rudwick, 86).

In 1866, black Baptists of North Carolina formed the first State black Convention. Other States soon followed: Alabama, Virginia, Arkansas, Kentucky, Mississippi, Georgia, and Louisiana. Note the southern states established their conventions before the northerners did. By 1880 every southern State had a black Baptist convention. We see in black conventions on a larger scale what is true in the black churches on a smaller scale. Politically, the local church is a microcosm of the convention. Black Baptists created their own arena in which to exercise political gifts and rights denied to them by white society. This development of the church, associations and conventions then was the response of the blacks to the closed door of American political institutions.

Notes

1. *Baptist Mission Magazine,* 1844, vol. 2, p 158, cited by Barnes, 23.

2. Jordan, *Negro Baptist History,* 26; Walter H. Brooks, "Evolution," 19, offers the year 1833. According to Fitts, 65, the date is *1834.* It is *1835,* according to Sobel, 216; *1836,* according to Pelt and Smith, 68, 83; Meier and Rudwick, 87; Satterfield, 73; and Simpson, 233.

3. Cf. Torbet, 354; Fitts, 66; Pelt and Smith, 84; Satterfield, 73; Simpson, 233; Brooks, 19; J. M. Washington, 31; and 1839 according to Jordan, 26.

4. Pelt and Smith, 84; cf. The Northwestern and Southern Baptist Convention of 1864.

CHAPTER 9

CONVENTIONS

African Baptist Missionary Society – 1815

Collin Teague and Lott Carey organized this Society in Richmond, Va., and remained associated with the white Baptist church there (Jackson, 24; Lincoln and Mamiya, 45). At this point, all black Baptist churches in the South were associated with white Baptist churches (Brooks, "Evolution" 17). Carey and Teague were sent by the Society to Africa in 1821, where Carey established the First Baptist Church in Monrovia, Liberia. From its inception to 1845, it contributed through a white northern organization, the American Baptist Union. When the white Baptists split in 1845 over the slavery issue, the African Baptist Missionary Society contributed from 1845 to 1880 through the Southern Baptist Convention (Lincoln and Mamiya, 26). The African Baptist Missionary Society also sent out W. W. Colley, who later was instrumental in founding the Baptist Foreign Mission Convention in 1880. He returned to America in 1878 when the SBC closed its mission stations in West Africa.

American Baptist Missionary Convention – 1840

This group was organized—the first black Baptist Convention that had *national* scope—in the Abyssinian Baptist Church of New York City. Concerned primarily with missionary activity, it gathered black church members from the New England and Middle Atlantic States primarily, but black southerners also attended the annual meetings. At that time, this Convention provided the only forum for blacks from various parts to meet (Sobel, 217; McKivigan, 107).

With limited funds, but with the help of white missions' organizations, the American Baptist Missionary Convention lasted some twenty-six years before merging in 1865 with the Consolidated American Baptist Convention. Its demise came as the result of the attempt to make every pastor a missionary, and every black church a mission station, regardless of age or strength of the local assembly. Worse, the American Baptist Missionary Convention sought to put pastors and congregations under the direct control of the Convention (Freeman, 62 ff; J. M. Washington, 38-42, 61).

Northwestern and Southern Baptist Convention – 1864

The Providence Baptist Association of Ohio (c. 1836), and the Wood River Baptist Association of Illinois (c. 1838) merged in 1853 to become the Western Colored Baptist Association, composed of thirteen churches in Missouri and Illinois. Reorganized, it became the Northwestern and Southern Baptist Convention, established to work in areas that the ABMC (1840) did not cover (Fisher, 107f; Pelt and Smith, 83f; Tyms, 147; Jackson, 26; Woodson, *History* 200).

Consolidated American Baptist Missionary Convention – 1866

Organized in Richmond, Virginia, this Convention was a merger of the ABMC (1840) and the Northwestern and Southern Baptist Missionary Convention (1864). The Convention refused to work with the Northern Baptists. To the blacks in this organization, cooperation meant subordination.

> They were unconsciously expressing the opinions of any submerged group which appropriates the culture and ideals of the dominant race or nationality and at the same time reinterprets them in terms of aspirations of their own. It is important to understand this racial consciousness to account for the progress of Negro Baptists (Fisher, 111).

By organizing the Convention into six distinct district conventions, the CABMC sowed the seeds for its own destruction. Each subsequent meeting showed signs of weak-

85

ening, until it met the last time in 1877 in Richmond, Virginia (Fisher, 110; Jackson, 27; Woodson, *History* 200; J. M. Washington, 79-105). Two of the six district conventions that grew and eventually over-shadowed the mother Convention were (1) The Baptist General Association of the Western States and Territories, which formed as fallout from the CABMC in 1873. It emphasized foreign missions; later the organization changed its name to the African Mission Convention of North America (Jordan, 64; Freeman, 64). They met triennially and represented nearly 100,000 black Baptists. By 1877, its membership had increased to 600,000 black Baptists, representing twenty States (Torbet, 354).

(2) There was also The New England Missionary Convention in 1875 that came out of the CABMC. The New England Baptist Missionary Convention or Society remains today, still supporting black missionaries and educational institutions (Fitts, 73; Brooks, "Evolution" 19). Concerning the demise of the CABMC, Dr. J. H. Jackson (27) comments, "It was literally consumed by the insubordinate and disloyal district conventions which had been established to help facilitate the work of the larger body and not destroy it."[1]

National Association of Free Will Baptists - 1870

Jacobus Arminius (1560-1609) was a Dutch theologian who believed that men have free will and therefore have the ability to attain salvation. The Arminian group who taught free will, free grace, and free salvation rejected the Calvinist view of predestination. Now the Baptist immigrants from England who settled in the colonies were of Arminian persuasion. One assemblage of this denomination arose in the South; and almost at the same time, another group arose in the North. Although there was no organizational tie initially between the two assemblies, they taught essentially the same doctrines (Brackney, 104). Paul Palmer organized a church at Chowan, North Carolina in 1727. In the North, Benjamin Randall (1749-1808), a former Congregationalist and popular evangelist, converted in 1770 under George

86

Whitefield, was in 1780 excommunicated by the Calvinistic assembly. He then established a congregation in New Durham, New Hampshire, in 1780. As zealous evangelists spread the movement throughout the New England States, they won many Calvinistic Baptists to the Free Will Connexion. They moved through New York and Pennsylvania, on into Ohio, Indiana, extending their influence to other parts of the West and the South, from 1820 to 1830. In 1827, a national General Conference was created, and that same year the Conference authorized the ordination of blacks into the ministry (McKivigan, 28). After an 1841 merger with the Free Communion Baptists, they were called Free Baptists. Their work in the South was limited because of the anti-slavery position they held from 1839 onward (Newman, 497; Satterfield, 47). Interest in the slavery question was first aroused among the Free Will Baptists through the voice of William Lloyd Garrison (Baxter, 93). Once alerted they vigorously fought for abolition.

McKivigan (28) notes that the Free Will Baptists were "second only to the Friends (Quakers) in terms of early religious antislavery prominence." In 1842, the Free Will Baptists organized the Anti-Slavery Society and by 1853 the denomination could report that there was not a single slaveholder among the 50,000 Free Will Baptist members!

By 1868, the denomination opened Storer College for freedmen, at Harper's Ferry, West Virginia. Other schools for blacks were established in Illinois and Missouri, but the Manning Bible School in Cairo, Illinois was the most notable. It merged with the Bible school for blacks at Nashville, Tennessee. In the West those blacks who considered themselves as Free Will Baptists petitioned for admission to the white Free Will General Conference in 1871 (Brackney, 243). In 1911, the northern group of the white Free Will Baptists merged with the Northern Baptist Denomination (now the American Baptists). However, still some 2,163 congregations with 186,136 members and 2,300 ministers did not join.

Then in 1916, "representatives of remnant churches in

the Randall movement reorganized into the Cooperative General Association of Free Will Baptists at Pattonsburg, Missouri" (Treatise). As for the southern group descended from Palmer, the slavery question prevented them from uniting formally with the Randall movement. By 1921 these southern congregations consolidated into a General Conference, but were unaffected by the merger of the northern group with the Northern Baptists.

In 1935, in Nashville, Tennessee, the representatives of the cooperative General Association joined with the representatives of the General Conference and created the National Association of Free Will Baptists (Mead and Hill, 54f). In 1866 a group of black Baptists with doctrine similar to that of other Free Will organizations, established the United Free Will Baptists with headquarters in Kinston, North Carolina. Shaw (217) gives 1870 as the date.

According to Fisher (132f), the blacks of the FWB separated and established in 1901 the United American FWB. With approximately 60,000 on roll, this is the largest group of black FWB.[2] With members primarily in North Carolina, Georgia, Florida, Mississippi, Louisiana and Texas, the General Conference meets every three years; there is also an annual meeting, and quarterly district meetings. There are other black FWBs across the land, but the splits that have occurred and the autonomy of the local assembly make it difficult to ascertain the total number of black Free Will Baptists there are in the United States.

Major beliefs of the Free Will Baptists (Baxter, 124-137) are: (1) *Free Will:* Man's will is free and self-controlled. Human beings have the ability either to yield to the prompting of the Holy Spirit, who is Truth, or to resist His influence and die. Man is a free moral agent. The believer who through grace perseveres unto the end of life has promise of eternal salvation. (2) *Imputation* of Adam's sin to the human race is rejected. Man is to be punished for his own sins. (3) *Tithing* is taught. (4) *Election:* From the beginning God determined to save everyone who complies with the conditions of salvation that the Lord set up. A person thus becomes God's elect by faith in Christ. (5) *Ordinances:* (a) Christian Baptism by immersion (b) The Lord's Supper. In direct opposition to the Calvinistic Baptists of the time, the FWB practiced open communion; they invited all Christians to partake (c) Washing the feet of the saints.

In keeping with their literal interpretation of Scripture, some Free Will Baptists practiced the washing of feet according to the example in John 13. At first this custom was considered an ordinance of the Gospel as much as baptism and the Lord's Supper. Some questioned its standing as an ordinance since Randall had not confirmed the necessity of its observance, and certain practical considerations, such as the contemporary practice of wearing shoes and boots which was not done in the time of Christ, also mitigated against its continuance. After about 1832 the matter was no longer discussed and the practice finally disappeared (Baxter, 136f).

However, among most of the black Free Will Baptists it is the duty of every Christian to practice this sacred ordinance at least once a year. Instituted by the Lord, it teaches the believer humility and reminds of the need for cleansing from sin daily.

Notes

1. Washington (*Frustrated Fellowship,* 79-87, 95-105, 109-131, 136, 138, and 140) gives CABMC large coverage; dates 1879 as the dissolution of the CABMC (105).

2. Deacon Vangrift Golden. In 1916 there were 13,362 Colored FWB: Weatherford, *Negro from Africa*, 321.

CHAPTER 10

CONVENTIONS (continued)

Baptist Foreign Mission Convention – 1880

When W. W. Colley returned from Africa in 1879, the Virginia State Convention sent him to urge black Baptist leaders who had a desire for a united national black organization, to meet in Montgomery, Alabama, November 24-26, 1880. Colley was motivated in part by his displeasure at the bad attitudes expressed by certain whites concerning missionary work among the Africans (Horace, 121). Immediately six missionaries were sent out to Liberia, Cape Mount County, near the village of Bendoo, to open the first organized Baptist mission station since Emancipation.

Freeman (69f) also mentions some disagreement between black and white believers with respect to treatment of the natives on the field. At any rate, one hundred and fifty or fifty-one messengers convened at the First Baptist Church in Montgomery and organized the Baptist Foreign Mission Convention.[1] Its headquarters was in Richmond, Virginia, and the Convention was committed to foreign missions and overseeing the "diffusion of the gospel of Jesus Christ on the Continent of Africa and elsewhere" (Fisher, 112).

Its executive board was really the Foreign Mission Board. The Reverend W. H. McAlpine of Alabama was elected president (Pegues, 327-332; Simmons, 524-529). Seventy-four of the delegates were from Alabama. The others hailed from Arkansas, Florida, Georgia, Louisiana, Mississippi, North Carolina, Tennessee, Texas, and Virginia.

American National Baptist Convention – 1886

The Baptist Foreign Mission Convention repeatedly turned down overtures to cooperate with the white Northern Baptists. Blacks who believed there was a place for a convention that *would* cooperate with the whites, met in the

First Baptist Church, St. Louis, Missouri, August 25, 1886. At the behest of the Reverend William J. Simmons of Louisville, Kentucky,[2] some six hundred delegates representing many States and Washington, D.C., convened with the stated purpose of unifying all black Baptists for missions in the United States, Africa, and elsewhere; and to foster the cause of black education. This meeting came when conflict between white and black Baptists was rife.

Blacks wanted complete charge of their own religious affairs. The establishment of black conventions was an expression of that desire. However, some blacks contended the race was not ready yet, they needed more time, more cultural development, more white guidance, a few more years of social up-lift—then we will be ready—but not right now! Still others asserted that the white man's insistence upon managing black religious affairs made him an enemy to black race progress.

In 1893, at a Foreign Mission Convention, held in Washington, D.C., delegates from three organizations met to form the Tripartite Union, or Tri-Party Convention, represented by (1) The Baptist Foreign Mission Convention, (2) The New England Convention, and (3) The African Missionary Convention (Western States and Territories). Nothing materialized from this meeting.

National Baptist Educational Convention – 1893

As mentioned earlier, relationships between the white and the black Baptists were not the best. While the American Baptist Home Mission Society (ABHMS) of New York and the American Baptist Publishing Society (ABPS) of Philadelphia were responsible for most of the educational and missionary work of black Baptists, the blacks had little or no say in the formulation of policy in the schools they attended. The first attempt of black Baptists nationally to direct their own education led to the organization of the National Baptist Educational Convention in Washington, D. C., in 1893. Its purpose was to:

Secure data and statistics of the denomination; to assist graduates of the schools in securing positions; to provide a fund for the assistance of promising young men and women; and to bring together the educators of the Negro Baptists (Fisher, 116).

In time, the desire to own and control their own schools resulted in the founding of (1) Simmons University, Kentucky (2) Selma University, Alabama (3) Arkansas Baptist College (4) Guadalupe College, Texas (5) Virginia Seminary, Lynchburg, Va. (6) Central City College, Ga. (7) Morris College, S. C., and others.

National Baptist Convention, USA
(Incorporated) – 1895

In 1894 three Conventions adjourned their meeting to convene again in 1895: (1) The Baptist Foreign Mission Convention [1880] (2) The American National Baptist Convention [1886] and, (3) The National Baptist Educational Convention [1893]. In September 1895, at the Friendship Baptist Church, Atlanta, Georgia, these three united to become the National Baptist Convention, U. S. A. (Pelt and Smith, 83). Dr. Elias C. Morris of Helena, Arkansas, was elected its first president. Born in 1855 near Springplace, Georgia, of slave parentage, Morris was working as a shoe-maker when called into the ministry. He served as a pastor in Arkansas, and helped to organize that State's Baptist Convention (Pegues, 353-357; Elias C. Morris, "1899 Presidential Address," 301, *African American Religious History,* edited by M.C. Sernett).

Specialized Boards were created: (1) The Foreign Mission Board, with headquarters in Louisville, Kentucky, in 1895, was a continuation of the old BFMC. (2) The Home Mission Board (3) The Educational Board was begun also in 1895 with headquarters in Washington, D. C. It was for the most part, a continuation of the old NBEC. (4) The Baptist Young People Union (BYPU) Board was organized in 1899, with headquarters in Nashville, Tennessee. (5) The Publishing Board, also in Nashville (6) The Benefit Association Board in 1903 in Helena, Arkansas. In 1900 black Baptist women established the Womens Convention, Auxiliary to the NBCUSA. Black women from all over the country united and "symbolized the highest expression of Black Baptist Sisterhood" (Evelyn Brooks, 314).

Though black men assumed the roles of leadership in the churches, associations and conventions, they would have had very little to lead or work with had it not been for the black Christian women. Even in the 1870s and 1880s the black women began to enter institutes of higher learning. Throughout the South they organized various societies in their churches, and in time these local church groups evolved into state-wide organizations that complemented already existing State Conventions.

It was in 1883 that the Reverend William J. Simmons, president of the State University at Louisville, Kentucky, launched the first Statewide Convention of black women. The organization became known as The Baptist Womens Educational Convention of the State of Kentucky. Women found outlets for their talents, recognizing that they held very little power in the decision-making councils of the male-dominated Conventions.

They were quite successful, making known their presence, and adding considerably to the ongoing of Baptist life. The names of Nannie H. Burroughs, Mary Cook, and S. Willie Layten are outstanding (E. Brooks, 71, 75, 313-317).[3] Approximately one million people, in about 8,000 churches, were members of the NBCUSA at its beginning. Nearly one half of these were in the Southern States, the rest in the Northern and Mid-Western States (Armstrong and Armstrong, 214).

There are at least four main reasons for the birth of this organization in 1897 in Washington, D. C., with the Reverend C. S. Brown of North Carolina as its first president. Organization took place in the Shiloh Baptist Church of Washington, D.C. First, there was the controversy over moving the headquarters of the Foreign Mission Board. The first secretary of the FMB, the Reverend L. M. Luke of Georgia, died, and the Reverend L. G. Jordan, pastor of the Union Baptist Church of Philadelphia, was elected secretary in October 1896. He moved the headquarters from Richmond, Virginia, to Louisville, Kentucky. Unfavorable repercussions resulted, as the brethren from Virginia and North Carolina voiced their disapproval (Freeman, 87).

The second issue concerns the relationship with the white Baptists in general. There were whites who sought to dictate the policies of black Associations and Conventions. As Woodson (*History* 259) suggests, we should see, in part, the growth of National Black organizations as attempts by the blacks to eliminate white control. Those who sought to continue cooperation with the white Baptists and broke with the NBCUSA were the "cooperationists". Jordan reminds us that many of those who seceded had been educated in the schools of the ABHMS. [4]

The third issue ties in with the latter point: The blacks decided to print their own religious literature and thus put the control of the future of religious education through literature into their own hands. Motives of the ABHMS became even more suspect when because of Southern Baptist protest the invitation extended to black writers was withdrawn. Remember, prior to this, all the Sunday School literature for the black Baptists had been printed by the ABPS.

When blacks protested they had no input, Dr. B. Griffith of the Society invited a number of blacks to write for its *Sunday School Teacher*. Southern Baptists protested, for they also had literature printed by the ABPS. The Society withdrew the invitation. At that point, blacks decided to establish their own publishing house. Both the Southern Baptists and black Baptists pulled out and became independent publishers. Blacks dissatisfied with this step removed themselves to form the Lott Carey Convention when the NBCUSA Publishing Board made its first report at the Convention in Boston, Massachusetts in 1897. The crash program to establish the Publishing Board was the final straw that tipped the scale, moving this group to secede (Pelt and Smith, 100).

Secretary Jordan (Freeman, 88) contends that one reason some people went with the Lott Carey group was that "many of the leaders of that group were being employed as colporteurs and Sunday School agents by our white brethren or teachers in the American BHMS schools." Blacks trained in these schools continued to use ABPS literature, ridiculing the efforts of the black Baptists as "the greatest travesty on Biblical literature" (Woodson, *History* 261f).

In addition, white influence was exceptionally strong at Shaw University in North Carolina and Virginia Union in Richmond. Attempts by the whites to dictate policies served only to widen the breach and move blacks to concentrate their efforts to build up the Virginia Theological Seminary and College at Lynchburg. In large numbers, leading black Baptists of North Carolina and Virginia, along with others, broke from the NBCUSA. Lott Carey Convention thrives still today in this area. At the Chicago Convention in 1905, an attempt to re-unite failed.

Finally, a fourth reason is that given by the Society (after pulling away, it renamed itself, chartered, incorporated as a Society, not as a Convention): Their main grievance was that the NBCUSA spent approximately 75 percent of foreign mission funds for operating expenses and spent only 25 percent of funds on the foreign fields (Freeman, 89).

The National Primitive Baptist Convention, USA - 1907

The word *primitive* should not be limited to the definition of crude, unsophisticated or savage. Rather, the meaning as used by this denomination of Baptists is "An earliest or original state, archetypal," derived from the Latin word meaning, "first, first of its kind." Thus, the Primitive Baptists identified themselves with the early Church, the primitive, orthodox, first, apostolic Church. Primitive Baptists are mostly a Southern group of Baptists with very little national impact because of their anti-missions stance. Their stand against missions earned them the title Anti-missionary Baptists. Other titles for them include Hard-Shell Baptists, Old School Baptists, Regular Baptists, Anti-Effort Baptists, and Square-toed Baptists. The anti-missions movement of the early 1800s spread in the West and in the South. Some Baptists joined the movement and by 1840 it had become a separate sect. Certain local leaders felt that the educated, professional types who hailed from the big cities of the East despised their work. There was also a genuine fear that missions' societies and boards would disavow the idea of congregational autonomy and take over the local assembly (Handy, 179).

Evangelism as such was not rejected, but the churches felt that missionary societies undercut the authority of the churches (Sutton, 23). It was believed too that giving salaries to missionaries corrupted the spirit of personal evangelism. In 1847, there were only 68,068 Anti-missionary Baptists compared with 655,530 Missionary Baptists. Most of the Primitive Baptists were in Tennessee, Kentucky, Alabama, North Carolina, Virginia and Illinois. Their headquarters is in Thornton, Arkansas. Because there is no central organization, it is not known how many members are in this denomination. It is estimated that there are 72,000 in approximately 1,000 churches (Mead and Hill, 59; cf. Shaw, 215).

Black Primitive Baptists worshiped with the whites until Emancipation. Then in 1865, black members of the white Primitive Baptist Churches of the South broke away. Under Thomas Williamson, the Colored Primitive Baptists of America organized at Columbia, Tennessee.[5] Another source informs us of a group of black Baptists who formed the Indian Creek Primitive Baptist Association in 1869, and in

September of 1870, four black Primitive Baptist churches were called together and organized. 1870 is given as the date of their first annual meeting (Sutton, 32).

In 1906, a national movement was initiated and became a reality in July 1907, when at the Saint Bartley Primitive Baptist Church in Huntsville, Alabama, there was organized for the first time a National Association of Colored Primitive Baptists. In 1916, there were 15,144 Primitive (Colored) Baptists (Weatherford, 321). Their name was changed in the 1940s to the National Primitive Baptist Church Convention of the United States of America, Inc., with headquarters in Tallahassee, Florida.[6]

While opposed to elaborate organizations in general, the black Primitive Baptists have local associations and state affiliations. For example, there is the Southern Old School Zion Orthodox Primitive Baptist Association, composed of churches in New Jersey, New York and Pennsylvania. Opposed to Arminian doctrine (Fisher, 135; Sutton, 12), their beliefs are Calvinistic.

Some of the basic tenets of the Primitive Baptists are: (1) Originally, Sunday Schools were not accepted as part of the church, but today there are those with church schools. Opposed to all methods of worship not spelled out in the New Testament, there was opposition to the use of instrumental music in church services. This is no longer true in all of the Primitive Baptist churches. Only among the Hard Shell Primitive Baptists, a much smaller group, are Sunday Schools, musical instruments, etc., forbidden. Those Primitive Baptists who consider themselves Progressive, the larger group, do not hold to such restrictions.

(2) Secret societies are frowned upon by some Primitive Baptists. (3) Centralization is opposed, for the Primitive Baptists strongly believe in the local autonomy of each church; congregational polity is adhered to very strictly. (4) Only two ecclesiastical offices are recognized: That of elder or bishop, and that of deacons. They must be men, so there are no women pastors.[7] Incidentally, the ministers are not given a salary. Certain women are elected as "mothers" of

the church, but this is an honorary elective position. It may be, of course, a base of power in our black Baptist churches (Sutton, 45-48). (5) Healing is important, but there is no highly organized, spectacular, indiscriminate healing. Personal, visionary experiences play a big part in their testimonies, and serve for the members as a source of spiritual knowledge. (6) Bible distribution groups are disdained, for if God has not given you the gift of understanding, then the Bible for you is a closed book. Nor do the Primitive Baptists force their own children to read the Bible. (7) Preaching is central, and "speaking in tongues" (*glossalalia*) is not practiced (Sutton, 101, 105, 170, 181).

(8) Concerning Election and Predestination: The true Church consists of a set number of people whom God chose to be saved before the beginning of creation. All others are abandoned to damnation. God's number is fixed; so there is no need for evangelistic campaigns. Fallen man cannot save himself. In conversion, God the Holy Spirit reaches out, in the Name of Jesus Christ, and claims that person whom God chose and foreordained; therefore, missions are not considered. God has decided already who would be saved, who would not. (9) Finally, on the matter of ordinances: Communion or the Lord's Supper is mandatory, usually taken once a month. Non-members do not participate in the Communion, however. If a member of the Primitive Baptist church takes communion with another denomination, he gives cause for dismissal. Baptism, is mandatory, and is by immersion. Most members practice foot washing, performing it at the same service when the Lord's Supper is observed (Sutton, 135-137).

National Baptist Convention of America, Unincorporated – 1915

Conflict between the white Northern Baptists and the black Baptists increased, especially during the years 1875 to 1896. Blacks became more resentful at not having more to say in the affairs of the ABHMS. Their strained relations gave impetus to the formation of the all black NBCUSA, and "the Northern White Baptists were partly responsible for furthering racial division within Protestantism" (Reimers, 58).

Three issues were: (1) would the whites continue to dominate black religious works? (2) What is the status of black religious leaders in programs controlled by the whites? (3) What Curriculum material would they use in Christian Education? (Tyms, 152). Dr. Morris, NBCUSA president reasoned that blacks should have their own publishing house for: (1) race employment (2) race development (3) bequest to posterity (4) a business enterprise (Morris, 56-58). There was great rejoicing when the Publishing Board put out its first issue of *The Sunday School Teacher* and quarterlies in January 1897. However, there was trouble ahead. The Convention assumed that because all Boards had functioned with the NBCUSA that the Convention owned and controlled them.

> The NBC, which had never been incorporated simply because with the fidelity to the principle of 'gentleman's agreements' it had never seemed necessary, was in a serious plight with a Publishing Board which was incorporated. The Board's refusal to obey the directions of the Convention could be supported legally because the Board was self-perpetuating, whereas the Convention legally died each time it adjourned (Jackson, 103).

Dr. R. H. Boyd of Texas was the secretary and treasurer of both the Home Mission Board and the Publishing Board. He was an astute businessman and his tenure was extremely successful financially. In fact, the Publishing Board was in the best financial position of any agent of the Convention. However, the Board made no financial contribution to any of the other organizations of the Convention, "no matter how dire the need for religious, educational, or mission work" (Freeman, 94).

President Morris recommended separation of the Boards in the 1905 Convention so each could have its own officers. Boyd fought it, and in 1914, Boyd resigned the Home Mission Board but kept his position on the Publishing Board. He had copyrighted materials in his own name, and built a new publishing house on property that belonged to him (Pelt and Smith, 103). When asked to make financial records available to the Convention, he refused.

Here was the conflict! Who owned the Publishing House, Dr. Boyd or the Convention that created it? From the Convention's perspective, the Publishing Board usurped the power of the body and put into private hands that which the members of the Convention considered Convention property. Boyd and the Publishing Board refused to obey the orders of the Convention. When the Convention met in Chicago in 1915 attempts made to settle the issue failed.

Legally Boyd was right; and the Convention discovered that it was not properly legally covered. The Convention had no formal hold on the Corporation that Boyd had formed in the State of Tennessee. Since the NBCUSA at the time was not incorporated, and could not legally elect members of the Publishing Board, it could not control the Board. However, it could refuse to accept the legal status of the Publishing Board. Since no mention was made of the Publishing Board having any affiliation with the NBCUSA, and the Supreme Court of the State of Tennessee upheld Boyd, an impasse was reached.

The result: Boyd withdrew the Publishing Board from the Convention, and with other dissidents organized the National Baptist Convention of America, Unincorporated, September 9, 1915, in the Salem Baptist Church, Chicago, Illinois. Dr. E. P. Jones of Mississippi was elected president. The courts gave everything to the seceding Board, so that "without even a pencil or a mailing list, the Convention started all over again." (Freeman, 98). Fortunately, however, for the NBCUSA, the rest of the Convention remained intact.[8] Concerning the split in 1915, Washington states it

Can be accounted for in large measure by external socio-economic pressures. With no higher loyalty than to the race and its progress, and with little or no success in advancing against the seemingly invulnerable common enemy, Negro Baptists turned their wrath and hostility inward upon themselves. The only channel at the disposal of the Negro for implosion was religion [9]

National Baptist Evangelical Life and Soul Saving Assembly of the U. S. A. – 1920

This group was organized by A. A. Banks, Sr., in 1920 at Kansas City, Missouri.[10] It was established as a charitable, educational and evangelical Convention, not as another denomination, but as an evangelical organization within the NBC of America. However, in 1937 it became an independent body (Lincoln and Mamiya, 21). In 1971, it was reported to have 57,674 members in 264 churches (Torbet, 543). The organization has its headquarters presently in Detroit, Michigan.

Negro Baptist Educational Society of the Northeast, Central and Western States – 1922

Organized in Chicago it is now defunct. Fisher (*Short History,* 121) suggests that had it succeeded, the NBCUSA might have become a Southern institution.

Progressive National Baptist Convention, Inc. – 1961

The Progressive Convention was organized November 4, 1961, in the Zion Baptist Church of Cincinnati, Ohio. Tenure for officers was the main cause of disagreement and the break with the NBCUSA, Inc. The conservatism of Dr. J. H. Jackson, its president, was another issue. PNBC adopted as its motto: "Unity, Service, Fellowship, Peace" (Lincoln and Mamiya, 36-39). Whereas Dr. Jackson refused to be engaged

101

with the Civil Rights movement, the PNBC supported it, and began an "active role in civil rights, social justice, and political causes" (Mead & Hill, 61). Headquarters for the Progressive Convention is Washington, D. C.

The National Missionary Baptist Convention of America 1988

Approximately 25 percent of the membership of the NBCA opposed the private ownership and leadership of the Boyd family of the Publishing House and over the Sunday School Congress. This group split from the National Baptist Convention of America in 1988, and organized the National Missionary Baptist Convention of America (NMBCA). "It sought an organizational plan by which the Convention itself would control the congress and publishing activities" (Mead and Hill, 57); cf. The Philadelphia Tribune, September 5, 1989, page 4-B, "Newly organized Baptist group convenes".

Summary

The progression was from association to State Convention to National Convention. White Baptists had their major problem over the issue of slavery. Splits in the black Baptist Conventions centered over matters of personal control, tenure of office, organization integration (relationship of a Board to the Parent Body); political position, relationship with whites, etc.[11] Doctrinal questions were not involved at all (Pelt and Smith, 102). Without doubt, association and convention life among the black Baptists strengthened the denomination greatly, and increased the influence of the church in the lives of black Americans.

Notes

1. Armstrong and Armstrong, 213. Minutes for this meeting: L. G. Jordan, *Negro Baptist History*, 153ff.

2. Fisher, 113f. Simmons authored of *Men of Mark.* Pegues, 439-453. J. M. Washington, ANBC (135, 138-147, 152-181).

3. Cheryl T. Gilkes, "The Politics of 'Silence'": "the overwhelming sexism among black Baptist men," 100. *African-American Christianity,* P. E. Johnson, ed. Cf. Dormetria La Sharne Robinson, "Nannie Helen Burroughs" *American Baptist Quarterly* 23 (June 2004): 155-178. Leonard, 277-80.

4. Cf. L. G. Jordan, *Negro Baptist History,* 320-325 for work of the ABHMS, and 326-331 for work of the ABPS.

5. J. R. Washington, Jr., *Black Religion,* 201. John Hope Franklin, 305. Carter G. Woodson, *History,* 192.

6. WBE, "National Primitive Baptist Convention in the U. S. A.": Has more than 1,800 churches. Lincoln and Mamiya, 21, estimate this denomination has 250,000 members. Mead and Hill, 58, estimate 1,530 churches with a one million membership.

7. There *are* women pastors in the black Free Will Baptist denomination.

8. Cf. Freeman, 93-99; J. H. Jackson, 105-107; and L. G. Jordan, 115-130, for detailed account of the problems.

9. J. R. Washington, Jr., *Black Religion,* 53. See Jackson, 117, for refutation of Washington's comments about the split.

10. Shaw, 214. No mention of this convention in Mead and Hill, 2001. J. M. Washington (200) suggests 1921 as date.

11. Winthrop S. Hudson, *Religion in America,* 353f: "other minor schisms resulted in the formation of the short-lived New Era Baptist Convention and the Progressive Baptist Convention."

BLACK BAPTIST NATIONAL CONVENTIONS

Name	Date	Place Founded	History
1. African Baptist Missionary Convention	1815	Richmond, VA	Lott Carey helped Organize
2. American Baptist Missionary Convention	1840	New York City, NY	Emphasis: Missions; Merged with Consolidated, 1866
3. Northwestern & Southern Baptist Convention	1864		Mergers: name changes & reorganization
4. Consolidated American Baptist Missionary Convention	1866	Richmond, VA	Merger of #2 and #3.
5. General Assoc. of the Western States & Territories	1873		Foreign missions emphasis; became the African Mission Conv.
6. New England Missionary Convention	1875		Fallout of Consolidated; support Black missionaries & Education
7. Baptist Foreign Mission Conv.	1880	Montgomery, AL	Displeasure with whites; unite blacks nationally
8. American Nat'l Baptist Convention	1886	St. Louis, MO	Unite black American missions in cooperation with whites
9. National Baptist Educational Convention	1893	Washington, D. C.	Uplift Education of blacks through the churches
10. National Baptist Convention, USA, Inc.	1895	Atlanta, GA	Merger of #7, #8, #9

BLACK BAPTIST NATIONAL CONVENTIONS

Name	Date	Place Founded	History
11. Lott Carey Foreign Missionary Convention	1897	Washington, D. C.	Dispute with NBCUSA over Publishing House; and cooperation with whites
12. United Free Will Baptist Convention	1870		Formally organized in 1901
13. National Primitive Baptist Convention	1907		Withdrew from white Primitive Baptist in 1865
14. National Baptist Convention of America, Incorporated, 1988	1915	Chicago, IL	Dispute with NBCUSA over ownership of Publishing House
15. National Baptist Evangelical Life & Soul Saving Assembly of the USA	1920		Split from NBCA became independent 1936
16. Free For All Missionary Baptist Church, Inc.	1955		
17. Progressive National Baptist Convention, Inc.	1961	Cincinnati, OH	Dispute with NBCUSA over tenure, more liberal social action stance
18. National Missionary Baptist Convention of America	1988	LA, Calif	Split from NBCA

Notes
1. Also called African Baptist Missionary Society. 3. Also called Western and Southern Missionary Baptist Convention. 5-6: were district conventions of CABMC. 10. According to Mead and Hill (55), originally the name was National Baptist Convention of America in 1895, became the NBCUSA, Inc., in 1915.

CHAPTER 11

Missions

Lott Carey

Prior to 1813, American Baptists did little to prosecute missions (Jordan, *Up the Ladder,* 47). It was in that year that whites formed the Baptist Society for Propagating the Gospel in India and Other Foreign Parts. In 1814, the General Missionary Convention of the Baptist Denomination of the U.S.A. for Foreign Missions was organized in Philadelphia, Pennsylvania, by 36 ministers and seven laymen (Barnes, 21). At the time, slavery was not an issue before the Convention, although there were churchmen in the North and in the South who opposed slavery

One year later, in 1815, the African Baptist Missionary Society was established in Richmond, Virginia. One of the founders of the Society was Lott Carey (or Cary, a spelling Fisher argues for). Carey was born a slave about 1780—no exact record of his birth date was kept—on the estate of William A. Christian, in Charles City County, about thirty miles south of Richmond, Virginia. Converted in 1807 under the white pastor of the First Baptist Church of Richmond, Carey was baptized into the fellowship of that church (Brooks, "Evolution" 19).

He taught himself to read and to write by memorizing Bible verses. By saving up money earned as a worker in a tobacco warehouse, where his master had hired him out, Carey was able to pay $850 for his own freedom and that of two of his children in the year 1813. In January 1821, he sailed for Africa from Norfolk, Virginia, along with Collin Teague, on the ship Nautilus (Brown, 18).

Carey was the first black missionary to Africa from America, representing a black missionary organization that operated outside the continental United States. In Monrovia, Liberia, in 1822 he organized the First Baptist Church. Today the same church exists as the Providence Baptist

Church of Monrovia. Carey died November 10, 1828, when a candle accidentally upset, led to a gunpowder explosion during an attack by unfriendly natives there in Liberia. Fisher ("Lott Cary" 417f) sums up Carey's ministry:

> From Charles City County to Richmond, from slave to freedman, from profligate to prophet, from sinner to saint, is a record that might have gone unnoticed; but from America to Africa, from governed to governor, from missionary to martyr is Lott Cary. [1]

Missionary Baptists

See the interest of black Baptists in missions in the names of their Conventions: The American Baptist Missionary Convention, 1840; The Consolidated American Baptist Missionary Convention, 1866; The Baptist Foreign Mission Convention, 1880. Use of the word *mission* informs one that the organization did not hold to the belief that there was no need of missionary activity because God would reveal His salvation to the elect, and no human help was needed. These Conventions were not anti-missionary groups.

> Our orders tell us to go and preach the gospel to every creature: That's why we are Missionary Baptists. A member of this church or any other Baptist Church who doesn't believe in missions or doesn't do something for mission is a hypocrite and is disobedient to the last orders of the Head of this and every other Baptist Church (Taylor, 11).

Despite Taylor's comment, the overall support of missions by black Baptists leaves much to be desired (Massey and McKinney, 50). According to one report, made in 1973, there were less than 100 black American missionaries among the 25,000 plus foreign missionaries sent out by this country (Plowman, 57). While Afro-Americans constitute approximately 12 percent of the U.S. population, they make up less than 1 percent of American missionaries. There are about 250 black Americans working full time in cross-cultural missions.[2] For the most part, they have been directed to Africa, the Caribbean Islands, and to certain areas of Latin America.

Black Baptist Mission Boards and Bureaus

The National Baptist Convention of America: The Foreign Mission Board of the NBCA has its headquarters in Dallas, Texas. One of seven operating boards of the Convention, its purpose is to foster the missionary objectives of the Convention in foreign lands. Presently the Board assists workers in (1) Haiti (2) Jamaica (3) Panama (4) Virgin Islands (5) Liberia (6) Ghana, and (7) Cameroon, where the Board sponsors the Dorcas-Luke Clinic.

The Progressive National Baptist Convention: In September, 1961, Dr. C. C. Adams, former executive secretary of the Foreign Mission Board, NBCUSA, Inc., called a number of men together in Philadelphia, and organized the Baptist Foreign Mission Bureau. In November of 1961, the PNBC, Inc. was born in Cincinnati, Ohio. At this session the Convention adopted the Bureau as its agency for Foreign Missions. Note the Bureau came into existence before the Convention. The Bureau has served in Haiti, Barbados, and San Andres; appeals have been made to the BFMB from Liberia and Nigeria, West Africa.

The National Baptist Convention, USA, Inc.: The Foreign Mission Board maintains Pre-School, Primary and Secondary Schools, Industrial Missions, Bible Industrial Academy, Medical and Maternity Clinics, Hospital for Women, Domestic Arts School, Christian Service Center, Seminary, Village Extension Schools, Churches, Extension Churches, and Missionaries. Their work is scattered throughout Africa: Liberia, Sierra Leone, Guinea, Malawi, Zambia, Swaziland, Republic of South Africa, Lesotho, as well as in the Barbados, Bahamas, Jamaica, and Nicaragua.

The Lott Carey Baptist Foreign Mission Convention:
This organization, started in December 1897, at the Shiloh
Baptist Church, Washington, D. C., presently has its Head-
quarters building in that city. The Convention meets annually
in various cities on the Tuesday before the first Sunday in
September. There are 16 States and the District of Columbia
affiliated with the LCBFMC. The Convention has work in
Guyana, South America; India; Liberia and Nigeria, Africa.

The Effects of Racism

In recent years, because of African nationalism, white missions boards have been forced to leave Africa or curtail their
operations. To some degree, the American whites themselves
are responsible for the limited numbers of black American
missionaries in Africa (Fitts, 120f; Banks, *Black Church*
101f). At the risk of being accused of ingratitude, one cannot
help but wonder if the white missionaries ever thought it
might be in keeping with the New Testament to train black
Africans to take over, to let the same Holy Spirit in the
whites lead the blacks?

Certainly to establish a work and then stay there forever
to supervise, instead of teaching, delegating authority and
moving on, was a mistake, an error blacks feel is born of
racism. Did it ever occur to the white missions boards to
train black American and use them as qualified missionaries
to Africa—prior to African nationalism forcing the whites to
leave? If the answer is yes, such thoughts were entertained,
then, it is a sad commentary concerning the policies of the
white Protestant missionary boards. Prior to 1900, the desire
to use black Americans was limited only by the failure to
find those qualified to serve.

At least 113 Black American missionaries [various
denominations] served in Africa between 1877 and
1900. The majority, sixty-eight, were in Liberia—
some of these had gone there as emigrants. This
contingent was followed in size by twenty in the

Congo, thirteen in Sierra Leone, six in South Africa, three in Nigeria, three in Mozambique, and one each in the Cameroons, Angola and Rhodesia [Zambia and Zimbabwe]. Of this total, fifty were sponsored by white churches and 65 represented black denominations. The black church agents were all concentrated in the Europeanized areas of the continent, like Liberia, Sierra Leone, and South Africa (Williams, 85).

After 1900, there was increased opposition to the appointment of black American missionaries. Because the Europeans had colonized nearly all of Africa, they felt any further attempts to Christianize, educate the Africans as the black American missionaries did, would only jeopardize the position of the colonialists, and create troubles. Pressure was brought to bear upon the white American Missions groups, and they acquiesced to the demands of the Europeans.

By 1900, the use of black American missionaries in Africa was discouraged. Concepts of autonomy, self-support, and self-dissemination of the Gospel gave way to paternalism, denominationalism and imperialism, ideologies born out of feelings of black inferiority and white superiority. In short, racism prevailed, and for nearly forty years—1920 to 1960, white American mission societies and boards excluded to the best of their ability black American missionaries (Jacobs, 20-22, 220). How shocking to read this!

However, such racism proved an incentive and motivation for blacks to organize their own boards, and despite lack of money, black Americans maintained an interest in African missions. In addition to racism, the shortage of black career missionaries may be blamed on a number of other causes, suggested by Plowman (57f). (1) Social history (2) unemployment, low income; poor economic situation in black communities (3) failure of churches to promote missions and educate their members, and to encourage them to support their mission boards with sufficient funds (4) young people need to be recruited and trained for full-time service. There is especially a need for black **men.** Black women have long played a tremendous role in Christian missions (Fitts, 121-134). (5) Finally, there is the lack of cooperative efforts, often engendered by the spirit of independence so typical of Baptist churches.

Notes

1. An excellent source for material on Carey, Miles Mark Fisher, "Lott Cary, the Colonizing Missionary," *Journal of Negro History,* 7, October 1922: 380-418. Also, A. W. Pegues, *Our Baptist Ministers and Schools,* 102-106; Wm. J. Simmons, *Men of Mark,* 506-509. David W. Willis, and Richard Newman, eds., *Black Apostles at Home and Abroad,* 211-242. Cf. Fitts, *The Lott Carey Legacy.*

2. Vaughn Walston, "Ignite the Passion," *Mission Frontiers,* The Bulletin of the U.S. Center for World Mission, 22 (April 2000): 14-16. I highly recommend *African-American Experience in World Mission: A Call Beyond Community,* 2002, Vaughn J. Walston and Robert J. Stevens, eds. Pasadena, Calif.: William Carey Library, PO Box 40129. Published in conjunction with Cooperative Mission Network of the African Dispersion (COMINAD), PO Box 9756, Chesapeake, Va, 23321.

CHAPTER 12

Doctrines and Trends

Early Black Baptists

We know little about the religious beliefs and doctrines held by the slaves in the early days, the seventeenth and most of the eighteenth centuries. In general, the whites simply did not bother to teach the blacks doctrine (Genovese, 185). Few of the black ministers understood the principles of the Baptist denomination. Illiteracy was a problem. Of the 409 members of the African church in Savannah, Georgia, perhaps fifty could read, and only three could write (Fisher, "Negro Baptist," 1). Elaborate catechisms and complicated explanations of doctrine were avoided.

Slaves did not have enough time for any real instruction. Sunday was their only day off, and often was crowded with the performance of their own chores: clearing ground, planting crops, family matters (Gaustad, 78). Still another problem was the ignorance of the slaveholders themselves. Yet, what the Baptist revivalists did teach about the Baptist denomination appealed to the slaves.

Du Bois (194) described a "typical church in a small Virginia town" as one where the minister fervently preached on topics like "Depravity, Sin, Redemption, Heaven, Hell, and Damnation." In short, the black churches became the heralds of the Good News that God in Christ cares, loves, and redeems all peoples. Belief in Christ helped the blacks survive throughout the centuries.

Tenets

In time, the principles of the Baptist faith constituted "the major thrust of the accumulated doctrinal context that was to become a part of the religious training of" black Baptists (Shaw, 3; Tyms, 102). Freeman summarizes these tenets which black Baptists hold, although admittedly the

112

NBCUSA took no formal action at any one session concerning these beliefs:[1]

(1) *Water Baptism:* Of course, slaves learned early about the ordinance of Baptism. They accepted and required immersion only, believing it best symbolizes or represents the death, burial, and resurrection of the Lord Jesus Christ. The candidate is dipped under the water. Sprinkling or pouring is not considered baptism. Some Baptist groups claim that the Lord Jesus was a Baptist, as were all of His disciples (Morris, 53). Only those old enough to make their own declaration of faith in Jesus Christ are eligible. This means pedobaptism, the "baptism" of babies is rejected (Newman, 1f).

(2) *The Lord's Supper:* The bread and the fruit of the cup or vine *represent* the flesh and blood of Christ. They are symbolic. Non-Christians and those not immersed are not invited to the Communion celebration. Furthermore, Baptists are not to partake of the Supper when unbaptized (non-immmersed) persons administer it.

(3) *Freedom of the Conscience:* There is to be no attempt to force another man's conscience. Men are to be free to worship as their consciences direct. As early as 1800, the black pastor, Andrew Bryan, wrote: "We enjoy rights of conscience to a valuable extent." Bryan appealed to whites to allow blacks to worship "according to the dictates of their consciences and in their own way" (Mathews, 200).

(4) *Separation of Church and State:* A free church in a free state is the ideal. Modern-day black Baptists seem unmindful of the struggle white Baptists had to establish this doctrine. The Episcopal Church, the State Church in Virginia, bitterly opposed the Baptists (Boyd, 65). Adoption of the First Amendment to the Constitution, September 25, 1789, is a monument to Baptists who fought for this liberty.

Today, black congregations—Baptists—readily accept government money for various building projects, preachers become deeply involved in politics, and church members readily go to City Hall in their suits against fellow church members—all of which are acts tearing down the wall of separation between Church and State.

(5) *Autonomy of the Local Church:* "No Baptist Church is subject to any authority but God, and sometimes it will disregard Him and run its affairs to suit itself."[2] Each assembly is independent, self-governing, free to worship as it desires, living its own life, choosing its own pastor, administering ordinances, disciplining members, with no interference from any hierarchy or other church or denomination. Of course, for the black churches in the South, there was no claim to sovereignty apart from the white man. However, after Emancipation, autonomy increasingly became a distinguishing mark of black Baptists.

(6) *Regenerate Church Membership* (Latourette, 960)*:* There was the common belief that man was a sinful creature. God the Father, stern but just, punishes sinners and rewards the righteous. But the only way to be declared righteous is through faith in the shed blood of Jesus Christ.

(7) *Conversion:* This was emphasized by the early revivalists, who leaned heavily upon an emotional appeal made to the slaves (Raboteau, 132). Thus the church is for saved folks, and the emphasis is upon the necessity of the new birth. (8) *The Authority of the Scriptures:* The New Testament is the guide of faith and practice. A literal interpretation of the Bible was held (Powdermaker, 230).

(9) *Otherworldliness:* What counts most is not the present life or the physical body, but the soul and the life hereafter. Powdermaker (225) points out that the Protestant churches of the eighteenth century were very otherworldly. Otherworldliness was not directed solely to the blacks; it was not peculiar to the religion of the slaves. The eschatological had an especial appeal to the racial temperament of the slaves, to that mindset produced by slavery (Park (127f). Plantation owners were satisfied with this emphasis since it helped remove any fear they had that the Baptist faith would incite to rebellion because of discontent with their earthly lot, the here and now.

(10) *Priesthood of All Believers:* There is an equality, a brotherhood among believers. All Christians have access to

114

God directly in confession of sin and prayer. (11) *Ownership* of all boards and agencies created or authorized to function in the name of the NBCUSA, Incorporated. Absolute control of such is in the hands of the Convention. This tenet is a result of the dispute over the Publishing House. (12) *Missions and Evangelism:* We are Missionary Baptists!

General Trends

Since 1916, black Baptists, like the rest of the nation, have suffered through periods of "rapid change, startling contradiction, serious troubles . . . great challenges and opportunities" (Brackney, 351). All Americans have been greatly affected by World War I, the Great Depression, World War II, the Holocaust, the Korean Conflict, the Vietnam War, and the shedding of American blood in Kuwait, Afghanistan and Iraq. We have suffered through civil disobedience, social unrest, and assassinations of leaders, Watergate, and a host of other events that point to a sad spiritual condition.

The fear of nuclear proliferation (and destruction) hangs heavy over us. There are such matters as crime, dope addiction, abortion, homosexuality, and alcoholism attesting to the lack of spirituality in our nation. The church is profoundly influenced by the breakdown of the family, the awful illegitimacy rates, and the increased urbanization of blacks.

Cities with more than half-black population are Gary, IN (84 %), Detroit, MI (81.6 %), Birmingham, AL (73.5 %), Jackson, MS (70.6 %), New Orleans, LA (67.3 %), Baltimore, MD (64.3 %), Macon, GA (62.5 %), Atlanta, GA (61.4 %), Memphis, TN (61.4 %), Washington, D. C. (60 %), Richmond, VA (57.2 %), Savannah, GA (57.1 %), Newark, NJ (53.5 %), Flint City, MI (53.3 %), St Louis, MO (51.2 %), Shreveport, LA (50.8 %), Portsmouth, VA (50.6 %), Cleveland, OH (51 %), Baton Rouge, LA (50 %).

Losses to cults, various Islamic groups, a general disaffection with the traditional church, and a nationwide secularism and materialism have hit black Baptists hard. In colonial days, Black Baptist preachers were poorly trained, however, the educational level has risen noticeably (Lincoln and Mamiya, 98f). The escalating cost of an education may slow the progress made in this area. As for theological orientation, the majority of well-trained black Baptist ministers are graduates of liberal schools. Only in recent years, the doors of more conservative institutions have opened for blacks seeking a theological education.

Integration

The late Benjamin E. Mays predicted racial labels such as Negro or Colored (or Black) will no longer exist as designations for denominations by the year 2000 (Reid, Introduction). Lomax (205) likewise waxed optimistic on this issue and speaks of that day when the "Negro Church" will soon fade away into the ecclesiastical melting pot, "a truly democratic society . . . a nation without an ethnic prefix." And if not integrated, the black church may disappear, states Washington (*Christian Century,* 472) because blacks will feel they no longer need the church in order to survive in white America. The emotional reinforcement provided by the black church will no longer be necessary.

However, there is little on the present scene that lends support to the possibility of the fulfillment of such predicttions. Not even the increased numbers of dually aligned churches will help erase the color line. Rising black awareness, increased participation in politics, celebration of a national holiday honoring Dr. M. L. King, Jr., styles of preaching and singing that so greatly differ from that of the whites, hinder church integration.

The growth of Black Theology, and Afrocentrism, continued racism and economic hardship in America—these issues weaken or make impossible any substantial degree of church integration. The black church will not fade away. Joseph Washington states that as long as there are separate black and white neighborhoods, there will be separate churches ("Roots" 127).

Unification

If we fail at racial integration, shall we succeed with unifying our conventions? In recent years, some of the conventions have combined their efforts in their missionary endeavors to aid the victims of famines, earthquakes, and tsunami. At a joint winter Board Meeting in January 24-28, 2005, in Nashville, Tennessee, four of the most influential black Baptist groups met. (1) The National Baptist Convention of the U.S.A, Inc., President William J. Shaw; (2) The National Baptist Convention of America, Inc., President Stephen J. Thurston; (3) The Progressive National Baptist Convention, Inc., President Major Lewis Jemison, and (4) The National Missionary Baptist Convention of America, President Melvin Von Wade.

Approximately 10,000 delegates attended the meeting, acknowledging economic and educational improvements as the two keys to improve the lives of black Americans. They set the common goal to put pressure upon the Congress and all the political authorities, to (1) reduce the HIV-AIDS epidemic (2) reform the Public Educational System (3) and create job opportunities.

Dual Alignments

There are black churches that belong to more than one of the National Baptist bodies. They cross national lines in order to cooperate with other blacks on state, associational or city conference levels. Indeed, in some areas, there may be only *one* black Baptist State Convention, composed of members belonging to the NBCUSA, Inc., and members of the NBCA, and members of the PNBC. The same is true in some cities of the local Baptist Ministers Conferences.

However, here we turn our attention to black Baptists affiliated with either the American Baptist Convention or the Southern Baptist Convention. Although estranged because of race attitudes and practices, whites and blacks often find themselves in theological agreement. In spite of past conflicts created by racism, paternalism and power struggles, in recent years there has been a steady increase in the number of black churches joining white Conventions (Fitts, 317). Lincoln and Mamiya (21, 414 fn 3) place black membership at 250,000 for the Southern Baptist Convention, and 400,000 for the American Baptist Convention.

In 1970, the American Baptist Convention and the Progressive National Baptist Convention invited each other to become members of an associated organization that would address itself to mutual concerns such as higher education, economic development, community organization, Christian witness, etc. (Brackney, 429).

Note that some blacks frown upon the dual alignment relationship, claiming it shows a lack of race pride, and the destruction of initiative that gives way to a *welfare mentality.* They also argue we should keep church property unfettered. Additionally, they accuse whites of failing to repent of past racist attitudes and deeds; they also lament allowing whites to rob black churches of leadership.

Ministers who are dually affiliated say that it is to their personal advantage. (1) There are increased opportunities for interracial and intercultural relations and fellowship (2) attractive health and retirement benefit programs (3) the possibility of loans for church construction and renovations (4) educational program and materials, and (5) disgust with black Baptist church convention folkways (Massey and McKinney, 88).

Separation of Church and State

Black Baptists are increasingly responsible for tearing bricks out of the wall that separates Church and State. There are those who see nothing wrong with pastors/preachers becoming politicians. "Seek ye first the political kingdom, and all these things shall be added unto you," is their motto. Often the preacher/politician has a membership that is large enough to support him as a full-time pastor. Those wearing two hats argue that their involvement in politics is an extension of their ministry. Notwithstanding, Paul admonished Timothy as a good soldier of Jesus Christ, not to get involved, entangled, in civilian affairs (2 Tim 2.4).

We see further evidence of a lack of separation in the use of church buildings as polling places at election time. Pastors and churches have readily grabbed government money in order to establish recreation centers, cooperative apartments, senior citizen homes, etc. Then there is the matter of litigation. We have seen throughout our study many splits. Black Baptists still sue one another; most of the litigation is carnal jockeying for power: Pastor, Deacons, Trustees, Musicians, etc., fight one another. They adjudicate such issues as defamation of character, tenure of office, authoritarianism, fraudulent elections, mishandling of money, and immorality. Our litigious spirit violates Christian brotherhood, and is in direct disobedience to First Corinthians 6:1-8. Church court cases continue, and the Baptist wall of Separation of Church and State is crumbling!

Full Gospel

On March 19, 1993, Bishop Paul S. Morton was consecrated as the First Presiding Bishop of the Full Gospel Baptist Church. He then founded the Full Gospel Baptist Church Fellowship, Inc. What are some of the characteristics and tenets of this group? Emotionalism plays a strong part; the practices of speaking in tongues and faith healing cause Lincoln and Mamiya (388) to describe the movement as a "neo-Pentecostal phenomenon."

The FGBCF maintains baptism by immersion; in addition, it practices tithing, and prayer and fasting. Autonomy remains. However, the explanation of the function of the Bishop seems to contradict autonomy, especially where there is a Bishop's Council, and certain members are called *Presiding Bishop, 2d Presiding Bishop, and 3d Presiding Bishop.* Although Bishop (function, to oversee) and Elder (rank) are titles for the Pastor, black Baptists traditionally have shied away from using them.

119

Though FGBCF claims it is not necessary for a church to leave its present affiliation, unfortunately, the appearance of "holier than thou" separatism has caused fellowship problems. "The Full Gospel Baptist Fellowship has had a tremendous impact on worship in many National Baptist congregations by adding a Holiness and Pentecostal veneer to standard Baptist theology and polity" (Quinton H. Dixie, *Frustrated Fellowship*, Washington, xix).

The Megachurch

Can a Baptist megachurch maintain the congregational polity that is essential to Baptist church government? Imagine moderating a business meeting of a church with 4,000 (or more) members! Is integrity and accountability maintained as the megachurch seeks to raise megabucks to pay the megamortgage? Will pastors of such assemblies create *microdenominations,* and find no need to have fellowship with smaller churches, conferences, associations or even conventions? Incidentally, all too often members of the smaller Baptist churches leave to join the Baptist megachurch, so that the phenomenon we now witness does not necessarily translate into increased numbers within the Baptist denomination.

The Purpose of the Church

Lawrence N. Jones (437) contends that in the future the local autonomy of the black Baptist church must give way to functional ecumenism. Such an idea strikes at the very heart of Baptist polity. Throughout the history of black Baptists, the form of church government has played a significant role. The same autonomy that enabled whites to observe more carefully the black church, appealed to blacks to have their own churches. If autonomy has prevented the kind of unity desired by Jones and others, who is to say therefore that such a polity is not New Testamental, or that it prevents spiritual growth? Is it God's desire that we establish some type of super church here on earth? What is our heart's desire, quality or quantity?

It is a mistake to teach that the Bible suggests the church will cause "justice and peace to prevail" among human beings. The true Church is looking for the imminent return of Jesus Christ. Only the Prince of Peace can establish universal peace; and even that peace shall not come until *after* a period of terrible tribulation, such as the world has not yet seen.

Black Baptists believe that the New Testament strongly supports the autonomy of the local assembly. Whatever shortcomings we have, whatever problems congregational polity creates, we must not violate what we believe the Bible teaches. L. N. Jones sets up an agenda for the church that is secularist and humanist to the core, when arguing for the use of church money to support cooperative business ventures to bring about social change. Unfortunately, his is not the only voice that cries out and demands the black church become more involved in political, social and economic schemes calculated to "make the world a better place in which to live."

Denominations aside, the Church consists of all who have faith in the shed blood of Jesus Christ. This definition transcends nationalities, denominations, political affiliations, races, and gender; in short, the Church is universal. **Positionally**, as God the Father sees us through the eyes of Jesus Christ, the Church, the body and Bride of our Lord, is perfect, without spot or wrinkle.

Conditionally, we are something else! Indeed, reading the history of black Baptists in America assures us we are a bunch of sad-sack saints in the sanctuary. The divisions, schisms, racism, and power struggles—all point to the weakness of the clay vessel that contains the treasured salvation. However, it seems not many church historians and sociologists believe that the Lord of the Church *never* intended for His Church to establish a kingdom on earth.

The Bible teaches Christians are to be salt, slowing up corruption; we are to be light, uncovering evil and pointing men, women, boys and girls to Him who is the Light of the

World. There are those, Christians and non-Christians alike, who disagree with this interpretation, even as Washington believes black Baptists have failed to focus "all of that potential power." Often critics are blind in failing to see that whatever beneficial social significance the Church has, it exists because of attempts to fulfill our biblical mandate, to witness Christ by living clean lives in a dirty age, and spreading the gospel of the shed blood of the Savior.

Who can deny the founding of colleges, the establishment of hospitals and clinics, and the myriad examples of the Gospel of Christ setting free captives of shackling habits, racist attitudes, and corrupt governments? It is amazing what has been accomplished by this piece-meal, individualistic approach. Attempts to unify black Baptists enabling them to wield a power that overwhelms evil and brings in utopia—or a heaven on earth—have all failed, and will continue to fail. One must recognize that the "tremendous fragmentation and frustration resulting from the various ingredients of a power struggle involving person-ality, and property as well as internal and external politics" (Washington, 203), have no surcease short of the second coming of our Lord to this earth.

Notes

1. Edward A. Freeman, *The Epoch of Negro Baptists and the Foreign Mission Board, NBCUSA, Inc.*, 84-86; Tyms, 97-102. See also L. G. Jordan, *Negro Baptist History, U. S. A., 1750-1930*, 107-109: What the NBC Stands For.

2. C. G. Woodson, "Things of the Spirit," 416, *Afro-American Religious History*, edited by Milton C. Sernett.

BIBLIOGRAPHY

Adams, C. C., *I Sat Where They Sat.* Philadelphia: Lyon & Armor, Inc. No date.

Adlam, S. & Graves, J. R. *The First Baptist Church in America Not Founded by Roger Williams.* Texarkana, Ark-Texas: Baptist Sunday School Commission, 1939

Allison, Wm. Henry. *Baptist Councils in America.* N.Y.: Arno Press, 1980.

Armstrong, O. K. & Armstrong, Majorie M. *The Indomitable Baptists.* Garden City, N. Y.: Doubleday & Co., 1967.

Bailey, Kenneth K. *Southern White Protestantism: In the Twentieth Century.* N. Y.: Harper & Row, 1964.

Baker, Robert A. *A Baptist Source Book.* Nashville, Tenn.: Broadman Press, 1966.

Banks, Wm. L., *The Bible and Black Slavery in the U. S.* Haverford, Pa.: Infinity Publishing.com, 1999.

_____ *The Black Church in the U. S.* Haverford, Pa.: Infinity Publishing.com, 2001.

Baptist Home Missions in North America: 1832-1882. N.Y.: Baptist Home Mission Rooms, 1883 (ABHMS).

Barnes, Wm. Wright. *Baptist Ecclesiology.* N.Y.: Arno Press, 1980.

Baxter, Norman Allen. *History of the Freewill Baptist: A Study in New England Separatism.* Rochester, N. Y.: American Baptist Historical Society, 1957.

Bayliss, John F. ed. *Black Slave Narratives.* N. Y.: Macmillan, 1970.

Beard, Augustus Field. *A Crusade of Brotherhood: A History of the American Missionary Association.* Boston: The Pilgrim Press, 1909.

Berlin, Ira. *Slaves without Masters: The Free Negro in the Antebellum South.* N. Y.: Pantheon Books, 1974.

_____ . *Many Thousands Gone-First Two Centuries of Slavery in North America.* Cambridge, Mass.: The Belknap Press of Harvard University Press, 1998.

Blassingame, John W. ed. *Slave Testimony: Two Centuries of Letters, Speeches, Interviews, and Autobiographies.* Baton Rouge: Louisiana State University Press, 1977.

Boyd, Jesse Laney. *A History of Baptists in America Prior to 1845.* N.Y.: American Press, 1957.

Brackney, Wm. H. ed. *Baptist Life & Thought: 1600-1980: A Source Book.* Valley Forge: Judson Press, 1983.

Brawley, Benjamin G. *A Short History of the American Negro.* N. Y.: MacMillan Company, 1913.

Brooks, Evelyn. "The Women's Movement in the Black Baptist Church, 1880-1920." Ph.D. Dissertation, University of Rochester, N.Y., 1984. Michigan: University Microfilms International, 1984.

Brooks, Walter H. "The Evolution of the Negro Baptist Church," *Journal of Negro History,* 7 (Jan 1922): 11-22.

_____. "The Priority of the Silver Bluff Church and Its Promoters," *Journal of Negro History,* 7 (Apr 1922): 172- 96.

Bruce, Philip Alexander. *The Plantation Negro as a Freeman: Observations on His Character, Condition, and Prospects in Virginia.* N.Y.: G. P. Putnam's Sons, 1889.

Brunner, Edmund de Schweintz. *Church Life in the Rural South: A Study of the Opportunity of Protestantism Based upon Data from Seventy Counties.* N.Y.: Negro Universities Press, 1969, reprint.

Childs, John Brown. *The Political Black Minister: A Study in Afro-American Politics and Religion.* Boston: G. K. Hall & Co., 1980.

Christian, John Tyler. *A History of the Baptists of the U. S. from the First Settlement of the Country to the Year 1845.* Nashville, Tenn.: Sunday School Board, SBC, 1926.

Crossing Barriers through Ministries with National Baptists, Atlanta, Ga.: Home Mission Board of the SBC, 1974.

Davis, John W. "George Liele and Andrew Bryan, Pioneer Negro Baptist Preachers," *Journal of Negro History,* 3 (April 1918): 119-27.

Day, Richard E. *Rhapsody in Black: the Life Story of John Jasper.* Valley Forge: Judson Press, 1967.

Dennard, David Charles. "Religion in the Quarters: A Study of Slave Preachers in the Antebellum South, 1800-1860." Ph.D. Dissertation, Northwestern University, 1983. Michigan: University Microfilms International, 1983.

Du Bois, W. E. Burghardt. *The Souls of Black Folk.* N. Y.: The Modern Library, 2003.

Duncan, Curtis Daniel. "A Historical Survey of the Development of the Black Baptist Church in the U.S. and a Study of Performance Practices Associated with Dr. Watts Hymn

Singing: A Source Book for Teachers." Ed. D. Dissertation, Washington University, 1979. Michigan: University Microfilms International, 1979.

Elkins, Stanley M. *Slavery: A Problem of the World Missionary Crusade.* N. Y.:Abingdon-Cokesbury, 1945.

Fisher, Miles Mark. *A Short History of the Baptist Denomination.* Nashville: Sunday School Publishing Board, 1933.

_____. "Lott Cary, the Colonizing Missionary." *Journal of Negro History* 7 (Oct 1922): 380-418.

_____."What is a Negro Baptist Church?" *Journal of Black Church History and Thought* 1 (April-May, 1983): 1

Fitts, Leroy. *A History of Black Baptists.* Nashville: Broadman Press, 1985.

_____. *The Lott Carey Legacy of African American Missions.* Baltimore; Gateway Press, 1994.

Franklin, John Hope. *From Slavery to Freedom: A History of American Negroes.* N.Y.: Alfred A. Knopf, 1988.

Frazier, E. Franklin. *The Negro Church in America.* N. Y.: Schocken Books, 1963.

Free-Will Baptists, A Treatise of the Faith and Practices of. Published by the Executive Office of the National Association of the Free Will Baptists, revised, 1979.

Freeman, Edward A. *The Epoch of Negro Baptists and the Foreign Mission Board: NBCUSA.* N.Y.: Arno Press, 1980.

Gardner, Robert G. *Baptists of Early America: A Statistical History, 1639-1790.* Atlanta: Georgia Baptist Historical Society, 1983.

Gaustad, Edwin Scott. *A Religious History of America.* N.Y.: Harper & Row, 1974.

Genovese, Eugene D. *Roll, Jordan, Roll: The World the Slaves Made.* N.Y.: Pantheon Books, 1974.

Gewehr, Wesley M. *The Great Awakening in Virginia, 1740-1790.* Durham, N. C.: Duke University Press, 1930.

Gillette, A. D. ed., Minutes of the Philadelphia Baptist Association, A.D. 1707-1807, Otisville, Mich.: Michigan Baptist Book Trust, reprint, 1976.

Glass, Victor T. "Working with National Baptists." Home Mission Board of the SBC, n.d.

Goen, C. C. *Broken Churches, Broken Nation: Denominational Schisms and the Coming of the American Civil War.* Macon, Ga.: Mercer University Press, 1985.

125

Goodwin, Mary E. "Racial Roots and Religion—An Interview with Howard Thurman." *Christian Century* (May 9, 1973): 534f.

Hamilton, Charles V. *The Black Preacher in America.* N.Y.: William Morrow & Co., Inc., 1972.

Handy, Robert Theodore. *History of the Churches in the U. S. and Canada.* N.Y.: Oxford University Press, 1977.

Harvey, Wm. J. III. "National Baptists in Foreign Missions." *Mission Magazine,* December 1968.

_____. *Bridges of Faith across the Seas.* The Foreign Mission Board, NBCUSA, Inc. 1989.

Hatcher, Wm. E. *John Jasper: The Unmatched Black Philosopher and Preacher.* Harrison, Va.: Sprinkle Publications, 1985.

Haynes, Leonard L. Jr. *The Negro Community: Within American Protestantism, 1619-1844.* Boston: The Christopher Publishing House, 1953.

Hays, Brooks and Steely, John E. *The Baptist Way of Life.* Macon, Ga.: Mercer University Press, 1981.

Herskovits, Melville J. *The Myth of the Negro Past.* Boston: Beacon Press, 1958.

Horace, Lillian B. *Sun-Crowned: A Biography of Dr. Lacey Kirk Williams.* Publisher; L. Venchael Booth, 1964.

Hudson, Winthrop S. *Religion in America.* N.Y.: C. Scribner's Sons, 1981, 3rd edition.

Hurst, David D. "The Shepherding of Black Christians." Th. D. Dissertation, School of Theology at Claremont, Calif., May, 1981. Michigan: University Microfilms International, 1981.

Jackson, J. H. *A Story of Christian Activism: The History of the National Baptist Convention, USA, Inc.* Nashville; Townsend Press, 1980.

Jacobs, Sylvia M. *Black Americans and the Missionary Movement in Africa.* Westport, Connecticut: Greenwood Press, 1982.

Johnson, Paul E. ed. *African-American Christianity—Essays in History.* Berkeley, Calif.: Univ. of California Press, 1994.

Jones, Charles Colcook. *The Religious Instruction of the Negroes in the U. S.* N.Y.: Kraus Reprint Co., 1969.

Jones, Lawrence N. "The Black Churches: A New Agenda." *Christian Century* (April 18, 1979): 434-438.

Jordan, Lewis Garnett. *Negro Baptist History, U.S.A., 1750-1930.* Nashville: The Sunday School Publishing Board, 1930..

_____. *Up the Ladder in Foreign Mission.* N. Y.: Arno Press,

1980, reprint.

Jordan, Winthrop D. *White over Black: American Attitudes toward the Negro, 1550-1812.* Baltimore: Penguin Books, Inc., 1968.

Latourette, Kenneth Scott. *A History of Christianity.* N.Y.: Harper & Row, 1953.

Leonard, Bill J. *Baptist Ways.* Valley Forge: Judson Press, 2003.

Lincoln, C. Eric and Mamiya, Lawrence H. *The Black Church in the African American Experience.* Durham, N.C.: Duke University Press, 1990.

Litwack, Leon. *North of Slavery: The Negro in the Free States, 1790-1860.* Chicago: University of Chicago Press, 1961.

Lomax, Louis E. *The Negro Revolt.* N.Y.: Harper & Row, 1962.

Lott Carey Baptist Foreign Mission Convention. "Fifty-Five Years (1897-1952) of Ceaseless Service to Others." Washington, D. C., 1501 Eleventh Street, N. W.

Lumpkin, Wm. L. *Baptist Foundations in the South: Tracing through the Separates the Influence of the Great Awakening, 1754-1787.* Nashville: Broadman Press, 1961.

Martin, Sandy D. *Black Baptists and African Missions – The Origins of a Movement 1880-1915.* Macon, Ga.: Mercer University Press, 1989.

_____. "Black Baptists, Black Americans and the Missionary Movement in Africa," 65. *Black Americans and the Missionary Movement in Africa.* S. M. Jacobs, ed.

Massey, Floyd Jr. and McKinney, Samuel Berry. *Church Administration in the Black Perspective.* Valley Forge; Judson Press, 1976.

Mathews, Donald G. *Religion in the Old South.* Chicago: University of Chicago Press, 1977.

Mays, Benjamin E. and Nicholson, Joseph Wm. *The Negro's Church* N.Y.: Arno Press & The New York Times, 1969.

McKivigan, John R. *The War against Proslavery Religion: Abolitionism and the Northern Churches, 1830-1865.* Ithaca, N. Y.: Cornell University Press, 1984.

McLoughlin, Wm. G. *Revivals, Awakenings, and Reform: An Essay on Religion and Social Change in America, 1607-1977.* Chicago: The University of Chicago Press, 1978.

Mead, Frank S. and Hill, Samuel S. *Handbook of Denominations in the U.S.* Nashville: Abingdon Press, 2001.

Mehlinger, Louis R. "The Attitude of the Free Negro toward African Colonization." *Journal of Negro History* 1 (July,

1916): 276-301.

Meier, August and Rudwick, Elliott M. *From Plantations to Ghetto.* N.Y.: Hill and Wang, 1976, 3rd edition.

Mitchell, Henry H. *Black Belief: Folk Beliefs of Blacks in America and West Africa.* N.Y.: Harper & Row, 1975.

Morris, E. C. *Sermons, Addresses, and Reminiscences and Important Correspondence.* N.Y.: Arno Press, 1980 reprint.

_____. "1899 Presidential Address to the National Baptist Convention," 301-313. *African American Religious History,* M. C. Sernett, ed.

Myrdal, Gunnar. *An American Dilemma.* N.Y.: Harper & Bros., 1944.

Newman, Albert Henry. *A History of the Baptist Churches in the U.S.* N.Y.: The Christian Literature Co., 1894.

Noll, Mark A. *Christians in the American Revolution.* Washington, D.C.: Christian University Press, 1977.

Park, Robert E. "The Conflict and Fusion of Cultures with Special Reference to the Negro." *Journal of Negro History* 4 (April 1919): 111-133.

Parvin, Earl. *Missions USA.* Chicago: Moody Press, 1985.

Pegues, A. W. *Our Baptist Ministers and Schools.* N.Y.: Johnson Reprint Corp., 1970.

Pelt, Owen D. and Smith, Ralph Lee. *The Story of the National Baptists.* N.Y.: Vantage Press, 1960.

Pierre, C.E. "The Work of the Society for the Propagation of the Gospel in Foreign Parts among Negroes of the Colonies." *Journal of Negro History* 1 (October 1916): 349-360.

Pipes, Wm. Harrison. *Say Amen Brother!: Old-Time Negro Preaching: A Study in American Frustration.* N.Y.: William-Frederick Press, 1951.

Plowman, Edward E. "Black Baptists: The Missing Missionaries." *Christianity Today* (October 12, 1973): 56-58.

Powdermaker, Hortense. *After Freedom.* N.Y.: Viking Press, 1939

Raboteau, Albert J. *Slave Religion: The "Invisible Institution" in the Antebellum South.* N.Y.: Oxford University Press, 1978.

_____. "African-Americans, Exodus, and the American Israel," 1-17. *African-American Christianity.* P. E.. Johnson, ed.

Reid, Ira de Augustine. *The Negro Baptist Ministry.* Philadelphia: H. & L. Advertising Co., 1951.

Reimers, David M. *White Protestantism and the Negro.* N.Y.: Oxford University Press, 1965.

128

Richardson, Harry V. *Dark Glory: A Picture of the Church among Negroes in the Rural South.* N. Y.: Friendship Press, 1947.

Richings, G. F. *Evidences of Progress among Colored People.* Philadelphia: Geo. S. Ferguson Co., 1904.

Roberts, J. Deotis. "Africanisms and Spiritual Strivings." *Journal of Religious Thought* 30 (Spring-Summer 1973): 16-27.

Robinson, Dormetria. "Nannie Helen Burroughs: The Trailblazer." *American Baptist Quarterly* 23 (June 2004):155-178.

Satterfield, James Herbert. "The Baptists and the Negro prior to 1863." Unpublished Ph.D. dissertation, Southern Baptist Theological Seminary, 1919.

Scherer, Lester B. *Slavery and the Churches in Early America, 1619-1819.* Grand Rapids: Eerdmans, 1975.

Sernett, Milton C. ed. *African American Religious History.* Durham, N.C.: Duke University Press, 2d edit, 1999.

_____. *Black Religion and American Evangelicalism: White Protestants, Plantation Missions, and the Flowering of Negro Christianity, 1787-1865.* Metuchen, N.J.: Scarecrow Press, and the American Theological Library Association, 1975.

Shade, Wm. G. and Herrenkohl, Roy C. eds. *Seven on Black; Reflections on the Negro Experience in America.* Philadelphia: J. B. Lippincott Co., 1969.

Shaw, Bynum. *Divided We Stand: The Baptists in American Life.* Durham, N.C.: Moore Publishing Co., 1974

Simmons, Wm. J. *Men of Mark: Eminent, Progressive and Rising.* Cleveland, Ohio: Geo. M. Rewell & Co., 1887.

Simms, James Meriles. *The First Colored Baptist Church in North America: Constituted at Savannah, Georgia, January 20, A.D. 1788.* N.Y.: Negro Universities Press, 1969, reprint.

Simpson, George Eaton. *Black Religions in the New World.* N.Y.: Columbia University Press, 1978.

Smith, Hilrie Shelton. *In His Image, But: Racism in Southern Religion, 1780-1910.* Durham, N.C.: Duke Univ. Press, 1972.

Sobel, Mechal. *Trabelin' On: The Slave Journey to an Afro-Baptist Faith.* Princeton, N.J: Princeton Univ. Press, 1988

Stampp, Kenneth M. *The Peculiar Institution: Slavery in the Ante-Bellum South.* N.Y.: Alfred A. Knopf, 1978.

Staudenraus, P. J. *The African Colonization Movement, 1816-1865.* N.Y.: Columbia University Press, 1961.

Sutton, Joel Brett. "Spirit and Polity in a Black Primitive Baptist Church." Ph.D. Dissertation, University of North Carolina at

Chapel Hill, 1983. Michigan: University Microfilms International, 1983.

Sweet, Wm. Warren. *Religion on the American Frontier: 1783-1830: A Collection of Source Material.* N.Y.: Henry Holt & Co., 1931.

Taylor, H. Boyce, Sr. *Why Be a Baptist?* Murray, Kentucky: News and Truths, n.d.

Throgmorton, W. P. and Potter, Lemuel. *Who Are the Primitive Baptists?* St. Louis: Nixon-Jones Printing Co., 1888.

Torbet, Robert G. *A History of the Baptists.* Valley Forge: Judson Press, 3d edition, 1973.

Tyms, James D. *The Rise of Religious Education among Negro Baptists.* N.Y.: Exposition Press, 1965.

U. S. Department of Commerce, Bureau of the Census: Statistical Abstract of the U.S., 1985, pp. 23-25.

Washington, James Melvin. *Frustrated Fellowship – The Black Baptist Quest for Social Power.* Macon, Ga.: Mercer University Press, 2004.

Washington, Joseph R., Jr. *Anti-Blackness in English Religion, 1500-1800.* N.Y.: Edwin Mellen Press, 1984.

_____. *Black Religion: The Negro and Christianity in the U.S.* Boston: Beacon Press, 1964.

_____. *Black Sects and Cults.* N.Y.: Garden City, Doubleday and Co., Inc., 1972.

_____. "The Black Religious Crisis." *Christian Century* 91 (May 1, 1974): 472-475.

Weatherford, Willis D. *American Churches and the Negro: An Historical Study from Early Slave Days to the Present.* Boston: The Christopher Publishing House, 1957.

_____. *The Negro from Africa to America.* N.Y.: George H. Doran Co., 1924.

Wheeler, Edward Lorenzo. "Uplifting the Race, The Black Minister in the New Society, 1865-1902." Ph.D. Dissertation, Emory University, 1982. Michigan University Microfilms International, 1982.

White, Charles L. *A Century of Faith (ABHMS).* Philadelphia: Judson Press, 1932.

Williams, Walter L. *Black Americans and the Evangelization of Africa, 1877-1900.* Madison, Wisconsin: The University of Wisconsin Press, 1982.

Willis, David W. and Newman, Richard, eds. *Black Apostles at Home and Abroad: Afro-Americans and the Christian Mission from the Revolution to Reconstruction.* Boston: G. K. Hall & Co., 1982.

Wilmore, Gayraud S. *Black Religion and Black Radicalism.* N.Y.: Maryknoll: Orbis Books, 1998, 3rd edition.

_____, and Cone, James H., eds. *Black Theology: A Documentary History 1966-1979.* Maryknoll, N.Y.: Orbis Books, 1980.

Woodson, Carter G. *The Education of the Negro Prior to 1861.* Washington, D.C.: The Association for the Study of Negro Life and History, 1919.

_____. *The History of the Negro Church.* Washington, D.C.: The Associated Publishers, 1921.

(WBE), World Book Encyclopedia, The. Chicago: World-Book Childcraft International, Incorporated, 1981.

Wright, James M. *The Free Negro in Maryland, 1634-1860.* N. Y.: Octagon Books, 1971, reprint.

INDEX

Illiteracy, 7, 13, 30, 112
Integration, 116f
Invisible Institution, 51, 68

Jackson, J. H., 25, 63f, 84-86, 99, 101, 103
Jasper, John, 57f, 63

King, Martin Luther, Jr., 116

Leile, George, 19, 26, 51,
Liberia, West Africa, 47, 84, 90, 106-110
Litigation, Church, 119
Lomax, Louis E., 35, 116
Lott Carey Foreign Mission Convention, 94f, 109
Lynchings, 6, 65, 77

Mays, Benjamin, 23, 31, 36, 42, 66, 116
Megachurch, 120
Methodists, 6, 14f, 20, 24, 27-30, 32-35, 43-45, 50
Missions, 24, 43, 78f, 84, 86, 90f, 96, 98, 106-111, 115
Mitchell, Henry H., 39, 41
Morris, Elias C., 92, 99f, 113
Myrdal, Gunnar, 6, 23, 27, 30f, 38, 43

National Association of Colored Primitive Baptists, 97
National Association of Free Will Baptists, 86, 88
National Baptist Convention of America, (NBCA),
    98, 100, 102, 105, 108, 117
National Baptist Convention, U.S.A., Inc. (NBCUSA),
    92, 105, 108, 112, 117
National Baptist Educational Convention, 91f
National Baptist Evangelical Life and Soul Saving
    Assembly of the U. S. A., 101
National Missionary Baptist Convention of America,
    (NMBCA), 102, 117
Native Americans, 6, 12, 20
Negro Baptist Educational Society of the Northeast,
    Central and Western States, 101
Northern Baptist Convention (American), 80, 85, 87f, 90, 98
Northwestern and Southern Baptist Convention, 83, 85